Graphology

Graphology

by Monique Le Guen
Translated by David Macrae

Ariane Books

Contents

Printed in Spain
Printer, industria gráfica, sa.
Tuset, 19 Barcelona San Vicente dels Horts 1975
Depósito Legal B. 40626 - 1975

Frontispiece: Athena writing (Greek vase). –
Below: Man writing on a tablet (early Greek).

1. Historical background.

Graphology is the study of character through handwriting. The word itself was unknown before 1868, when a French priest, Abbé Michon, invented it and drew up a methodical system in application of it. Since that time; graphology has made rapid strides, and won many devotees.

It has always been somehow felt that handwriting should be able to provide useful guidance as to the character of a person. Suetonius made a graphological comment on the handwriting of Augustus: "One thing I have noticed about his handwriting is that he leaves no space between the words, and that, rather than carrying surplus letters forward from one line to the next, he places them immediately beneath the end of the line, and draws a line around them."

No other documents relating to graphology are to be found until the 17th century; and the reason for this hiatus is easy to explain. In Antiquity and the Middle Ages, few people wrote at all; kings and emperors often did not know how to write: there were public scribes who, since they had nothing to say of their own, but merely wrote down the thoughts of others, had adopted a characterless, official, calligraphic style. A brief passage occurs in a French book, in 1609, which is implicitly about graphology. It comes in the *Avis pour juger des in-*

scriptions en faux, by Francois Demelle, and which is intended, in the author's words, "as a way of comparing handwriting and signatures as a guide to practice, and as a way of detecting forgeries." He argued that handwriting reveals a person's character just as well as physiognomony. However, the true founder of graphology seems to have been the Italian Camillo Baldo, who clearly showed the possibility of studying methodically the relationship between a person's nature and his handwriting. Baldo left a very interesting book, entitled: *Trattato come de una littera, issiva si cognoscamo la natura e qualita dello scrittore* (1622; printed in 1662).

Some years later, the *Mercure galant* for October 1678 contains a letter dealing with the "indications provided by the way individuals form their handwriting". The text is rather general, though it does make some fairly correct, precise comments about signs suggesting avarice, sensuality and laziness. Leibniz should also be counted among the precursors of graphology. He wrote: "With few exceptions, handwriting expresses, in one way or another, a person's natural temperament, unless it is the work of a master, and in some cases even then."

Late in the 18th century, Lavater began his work on graphology; on the advice of Goethe, he began to collect autographs and study them: his aim was to draw the attention of the public to the striking similarity between carriage, language and handwriting. The result of his observations was published in his *Art of knowing men*, the first German edition of which appeared in 1775; a dozen or so pages of it are devoted to handwriting; however, his observations are general, ill-coordinated and somewhat vague. Early in the 19th century, Hocquart published a book entitled *The Art of judging the character of men through their writing* (1816). This book, now very rare, contains 24 plates, with the handwriting of various distinguished people; a number of his observations are extremely interesting. Another nineteenth-century work on the subject is Byerley's *On Characteristic Signatures* (1823). This work deals solely with signatures.

In 1863, Adolf Henz published, in Leipzig, a work entitled *Die Chirogrammatomancie, oder Lehre der Handschriftandeutung*, containing more than a thousand facsimiles, and a certain number of general ideas, but without presenting any general method for the study of graphology. For the most part, it merely reproduced enquiries which the author had published in the *Illustrierte Zeitung*, of Leipzig, and in which he had sought to draw a portrait of the person involved, from a study of his or her handwriting.

Later in the century; patient and methodical observers were to assemble the mass of confused observations made by early graphologists, and to put them in some kind of clear order. One of the more noteworthy of these publications was the *Practical Treatise on Graphology* (undated), and *Handwriting and Character* (1899), by Crépieux-Jamin, a dentist from Rouen; in them, the reader will find a thoroughly verified classification, in highly useful table form, of the all the signs whose meaning was known at that time. These two books stirred up a considerable amount of interest, and were translated into many languages.

More recently, Max Pulver, of Switzerland, and Ludwig Klages, of Germany, have acquired a well-merited reputation in our sub-

Below: the age-old symbol of writing . . .

ject. Klages, for example, has stated that his aim is to transform graphology into a science of the soul. Without refuting Crépieux-Jamin (whose wide following he recognizes), he intends to take this subject beyond the levels of "fifty years ago"; however, apart from a number of penetrating views, some of his findings do seem rather woolly.

2. General.

Broadly speaking, the relationship between handwriting and the writer himself are undeniable; there are as many different types of handwriting as there are people; moreover, for each individual, the handwriting can be seen to change with each major change in health, age or circumstances. Graphology is instinctive, each one of us readily recognizes the identity of a correspondent from the writing on the envelope. Moreover, a large, awkward hand is a sure sign of a child, just as much as a hesitant, trembling hand indicates an old person, while bizarre letters with lots of flourishes are the work of a pretentious person. The role of graphology has been to develop and refine these observations.

The objections which are commonly made about graphology are easy to refute; however, some comment is needed on them. One of the most frequent objections is that everyone can change their own handwriting in an infinite variety of ways. Yet, if one examines closely the various specimens of a person's hand, one is forced to the conclusion that such changes are only apparent, and that the basic features remain the same. Another claim is that it is easy to disguise one's handwriting, and thus to hide its nature from the searching eye of the graphologist. Here again, a sincere observer will find the same basic features of the normal hand recurring in the feigned style; although some of them will have been changed deliberately, others will not have been noticed by the forger himself, and will betray his trickery. Another objection has to do with national differences of handwriting; the British are said to have one style, the French another, and so on. But this argument is favorable to graphology: each nation has special characteristics which should surely find their way into the handwriting of a given nationality, and distinguish it from all the others.

A doctor has given a clear definition of the physiological and psychological bases of graphology. For some years now, the attention of philosophers and doctors has been directed towards phenomena which are regarded as being unconscious manifestations of the personality. The spontaneous movements of the hand, caused by certain types of cerebral activity, have been isolated; it would also be highly interesting to observe closely and methodically the unconscious movement of the muscles of the face, and its influence on the formation and final configuration of the facial features.

Just as it is beyond dispute that the characteristics of the personality are reflected in the face, there are other movements, such as gestures, the study of which is equally valuable. Nobody would challenge the notion that a person's carriage is a valuable guide to character, especially when the person's face cannot be seen. The number, speed and breadth of a person's movements all contribute to one's knowledge of that person. Speech is another sphere in which psychological analysis can tell much about an individual. In all these apparently different studies, the subject will be seen to be substantially the same. Muscular activity, in its various forms, is what is involved: facial movements, gestures with the arms, the motion of the legs, one's manner of speaking—all consist essentially of the action of muscles, partly voluntary and conscious, partly involuntary and unconscious. In its broadest sense the word *gesture* expresses these different modes of activity; a study in depth of these special manifestations of cerebral activity might help us attain a complete knowledge of the human personality.

"There is one piece of motor apparatus which is really more closely linked than the others to the ideo-motor cerebral function; its activities must, therefore, be a very faithful reflection of the various forms of that activity: that is, the apparatus of writing." Handwriting is a mode of gesture, being itself composed of countless tiny gestures. As it is beyond dispute that people give themselves away by barely perceptible contractions of facial muscles, by change in the tone of their voice or by a particular form of gait, it is not possible to deny that the movements of a hand engaged in the act of writing are also influenced, and even more directly, by the ideas and passions of the person writing. The important point is that the characters formed by handwriting are permanent signs, whereas other types of gesture are more fleeting, and more difficult to fix in one's memory. These gestures cannot be studied without an infinitely sensitive recording device, whereas, in the act of writing, the paper over which the pen moves is itself a continuous recording device.

These different considerations prove that attempts to read various characteristics of the writer's personality in his handwriting are no idle fantasy. Graphology is now seen to consist of the study of a series of unconscious manifestations of the personality in general, in other words the study of the signs which, through the machinery of handwriting, make them perceptible to the senses. Its foundation lies in the simplest and most indisputable facts of physiology, that is to say, the production of surplus nervous activity during thought processes, and its discharge in the form of muscular contraction. It falls entirely within the province of physiological psychology.

Let us take handwriting at its point of departure. No man is built in exactly the same way as another; using the same instrument, writing the same words, each of us will have a different handwriting, distinguishing the special form of our thoughts and sensations. It does indeed seem astonishing that, even though all children are taught to write from identical models, their handwriting varies to such an extent that, from the very first lines, each child's writing can be easily distinguished from the rest. These differences grow with the passage of time, as the individual develops, with the result that it is impossible to confuse one hand with another. It has been found that the curves forming calligraphic letters are equally divided between those which curve to the left and those which curve to the right. It has also been discovered that we do not all share the same aptitude for moving the pen from right to left and left to right; some shapes give us real difficulty, while others fall more naturally within our muscular habits. The result is that, within a short time, we have eliminated from our handwriting those movements which are awkward for us, and emphasized those which come naturally. These unconscious modifications explain the differences in handwriting, and the personal nature of each individual style. On the basis of

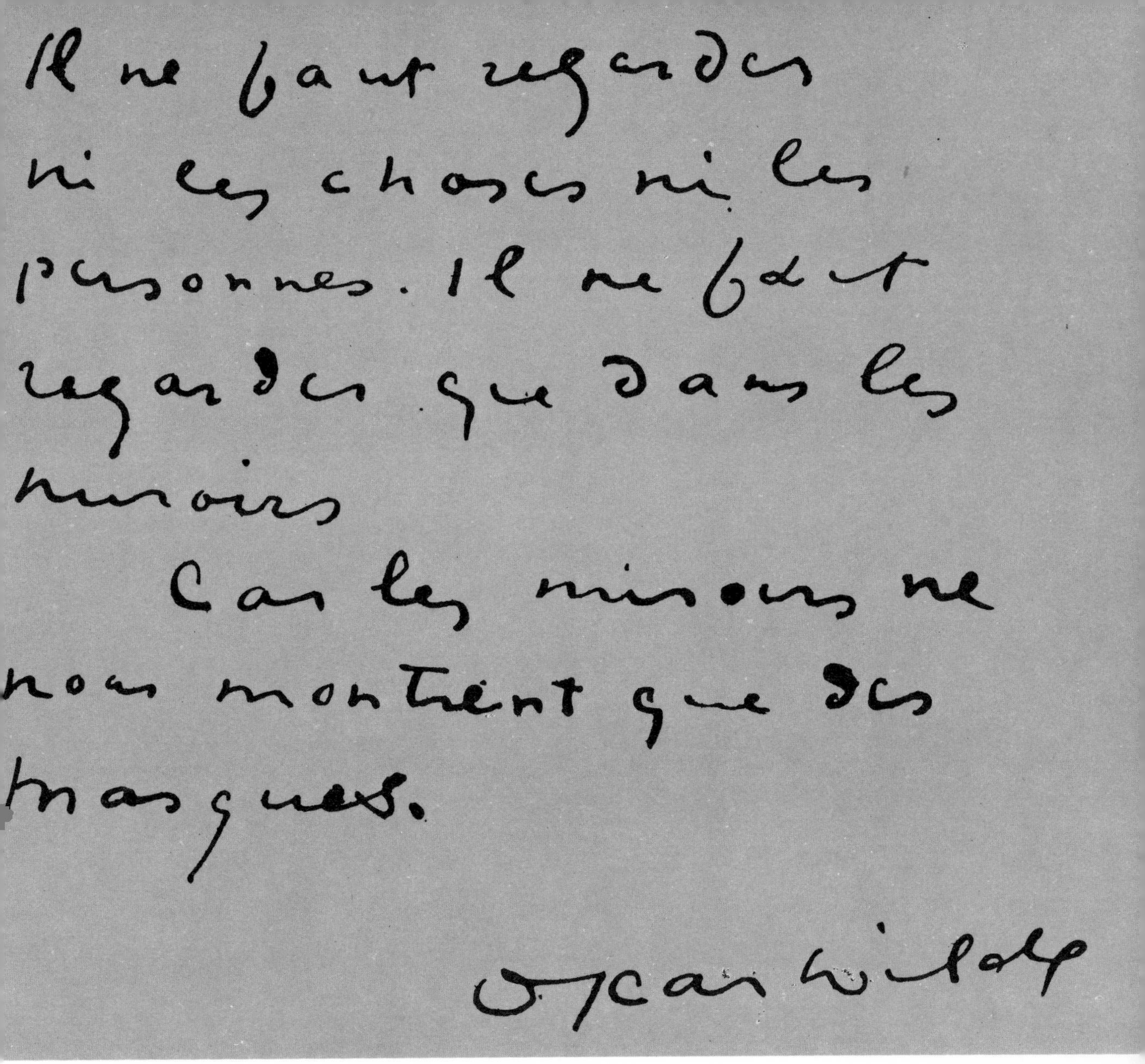
Il ne faut regarder
ni les choses ni les
personnes. Il ne faut
regarder que dans les
miroirs
Car les miroirs ne
nous montrent que des
masques.
Oscar Wilde

this principle, handwriting has been divided into styles in which the letters are curved from left to right, or *dextral*, and those which go from right to left, or *sinistral*; so far, no one has determined exactly whether certain traits of the character correspond to either one of these two tendencies.

Above: Sample of the handwriting of Oscar Wilde. Clear, relaxed hand, with lines and words well spaced out; yet, the overall effect is made somewhat heavy by a number of clubbed strokes and blotches. Wilde's aestheticism is willing to concede more to sensuality than to sensitivity, and is more likely to delve deep into the material world than to soar to poetic heights.

3. The conditions for thorough study.

By what means can one discover, with the greatest measure of certainty, the character of a man from his handwriting? Broadly speaking, the student should examine a great number of known samples of handwriting before attempting an original graphological portrait, as this exercise serves to sharpen the powers of observation. A knowledge of psychology is also necessary, and makes it possible to pin down the varying shades of emphasis in a character. A precise knowledge of the known graphological signs and their classification is a further pre-requisite. Assuming that the student is well versed in the graphological signs and in psychology, what precautions should he take when studying a given specimen of handwriting?

1. The sample to be analyzed must be *plain and natural*; although it is fairly easy to distinguish a forgery, and to detect signs of character in it, it is preferable to be working on a sincere dociment. A distinction needs to be drawn, moreover, between habitual and natural writing: professional requirements, for example, in office work, cause a number of people to adopt a special, legible, fast and quite insignificant style of handwriting. It cannot be said that it is a *bad* style, but it is often quite different from the personal hand.

Artifical, "display"-type handwriting is exceedingly common. Many public figures, whose lives are continuously involved with those of a great many people, have put up an impenetrable barrier, by using a calligraphic hand, so as to give nothing away, and reveal nothing of their passions, habits, etc. In these cases, it is the figure, rather than the man, who is doing the writing.

Here is an irrefutable demonstration of the capital difference between natural and artifical styles of handwriting (fig. 200 and 300).

Whoever would have thought that these two letters were written by the same hand? Such, however, is the case.

The sensitive side of the soul had completely disappeared in the first sample, only to emerge, emphatically, in the second.

2. You must ask the same person for *several autographs*, and even for letters dating from different periods. There are a number of factors which can affect the style of handwriting: the cold, a bad pen, an uncomfortable position, etc. Illness and convalescence also have a profound effect on handwriting. A person's true style emerges almost without fail in his signature.

General rules for the interpretation of signs. (signs meaning the particular shape of lines, words and letters.) As soon as a letter departs from the calligraphic standard, the differing feature constitutes a sign; for example, in the letter d with scrolls, the scroll is a sign.

Handwriting obeys the general law of proportions. The first thing that we notice about any object we see is its proportions; we notice whether those proportions are harmonious, neither too small nor too big. Clearly, there can be no absolute standard for the height, width and spacing of words and letters, yet there is a mean which seems to us harmo-

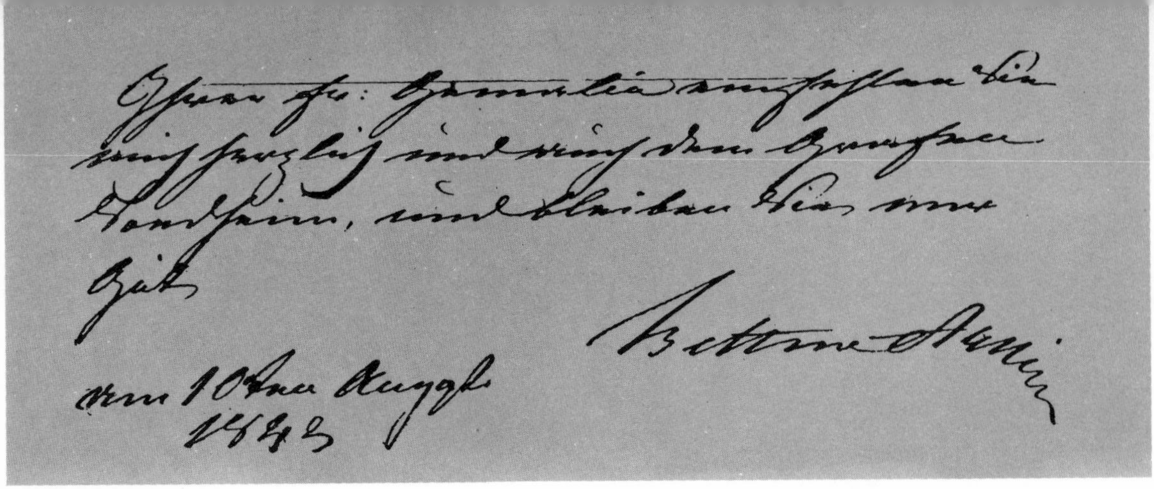

nious, and which serves as a criterion for assessing the value of individual variations.

Another clear principle is that of the *correlation of forms*; each shape in a hand may be deduced from the others. Angular handwriting is that in which the links between the downstrokes and between the letters are at an acute angle to the body of the letter. In the light of the correlation of forms, the body of the letter cannot be curved in an angular hand. On the basis of this principle, natural spontaneous handwriting can be distinguished from the artificial style sometimes used out of professional necessity, for example.

The meaning of features of a given hand are to be considered as the *material expression of a cerebral movement*. Thus, fast handwriting is a response to lively nervous excitement, clear writing is a sign of order, etc.

The general theory explained above will be seen to contain the details of this investigative procedure. Constant gestures and general signs in a hand reflect a constant and general feature of the character; special gestures and intermittent signs reflect a particular and intermittent trait of the mind. The intensity of a sign can be assessed by measuring it against the smallest and the biggest manifestations of that sign commonly found in a person's hand. As the reader will doubtless have observed, when writing a love letter, he will used a more sloping hand than when writing a business letter.

The human organism often reacts identically in different psychological states; in the same way, a *single graphological sign may represent different character traits*. People sometimes laugh to the point of tears, while great grief can bring on a fit of convulsive laughter. Let us take an ascending hand, for example: it signifies ardor, and also means ambition; a probable accessory meaning of activity is good humor; another possible meaning is the hope which stimulates the mind and produces a certain ardor. Of course, what is, for a superior man, ambition, would be mere ridiculous vanity in an ordinary mortal. Thus we have a whole series of meanings for a single mode of handwriting; and this example could be multiplied infinitely.

Inversely, a *single character trait may be rendered by several signs*, and, if a sign is seen to be *absent, it is not possible to conclude therefrom that a quality contrary to that normally expressed by that sign will be found in that person*. Vivacity, for example, is often reflected in long cross-strokes on the letter *t*, and also by a shorter cross-stroke ending in a point. Fast writing and, in certain cases, spindle-shaped words, the ends of which are barely finished, are also a sign of vivacity. Firmness can be detected in rigid, vertical or angular handwriting, by a highly distinct cross-stroke on the *t*, or one which is joined at the base; it is also represented by heavy emphasis. If none of these occurs in a hand, it is probable that the person involved lacks firmness of character; however, if no sign contrary to firmness is found, one cannot be sure as to the truth of one's findings.

According to Crépieux-Jamin, *any sign which is not repeated*, or the value of which is not confirmed by other, similar signs, *must be considered as invalid*. However, the value of a graphological observation is greatest if parallel findings are obtained from a combination of signs. The net outcome of these various considerations is that the meaning of signs may vary and may depend on the signifiance of the other signs. When considered in isola-

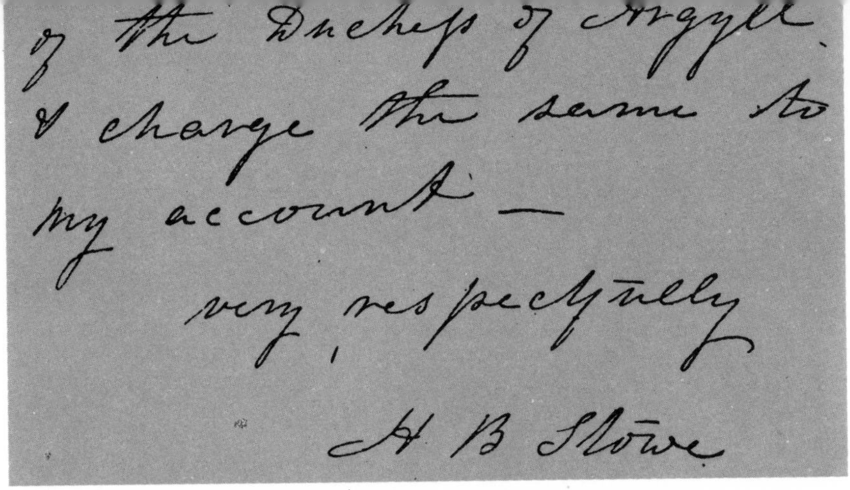

of the Duchess of Argyll.
& charge the same to
my account —
very respectfully
H B Stowe

Left: Some lines by Bettina von Arnim. An impassioned woman, of immense integrity, but difficult character.

Facing: Handwriting of Mrs. Beecher-Stowe: a sensitive, clear and open mind, coupled with great generosity, predestined her to be the champion of the oppressed. This hand belongs to a woman who felt duty-bound to pour her whole heart into the writing of "Uncle Tom's Cabin".

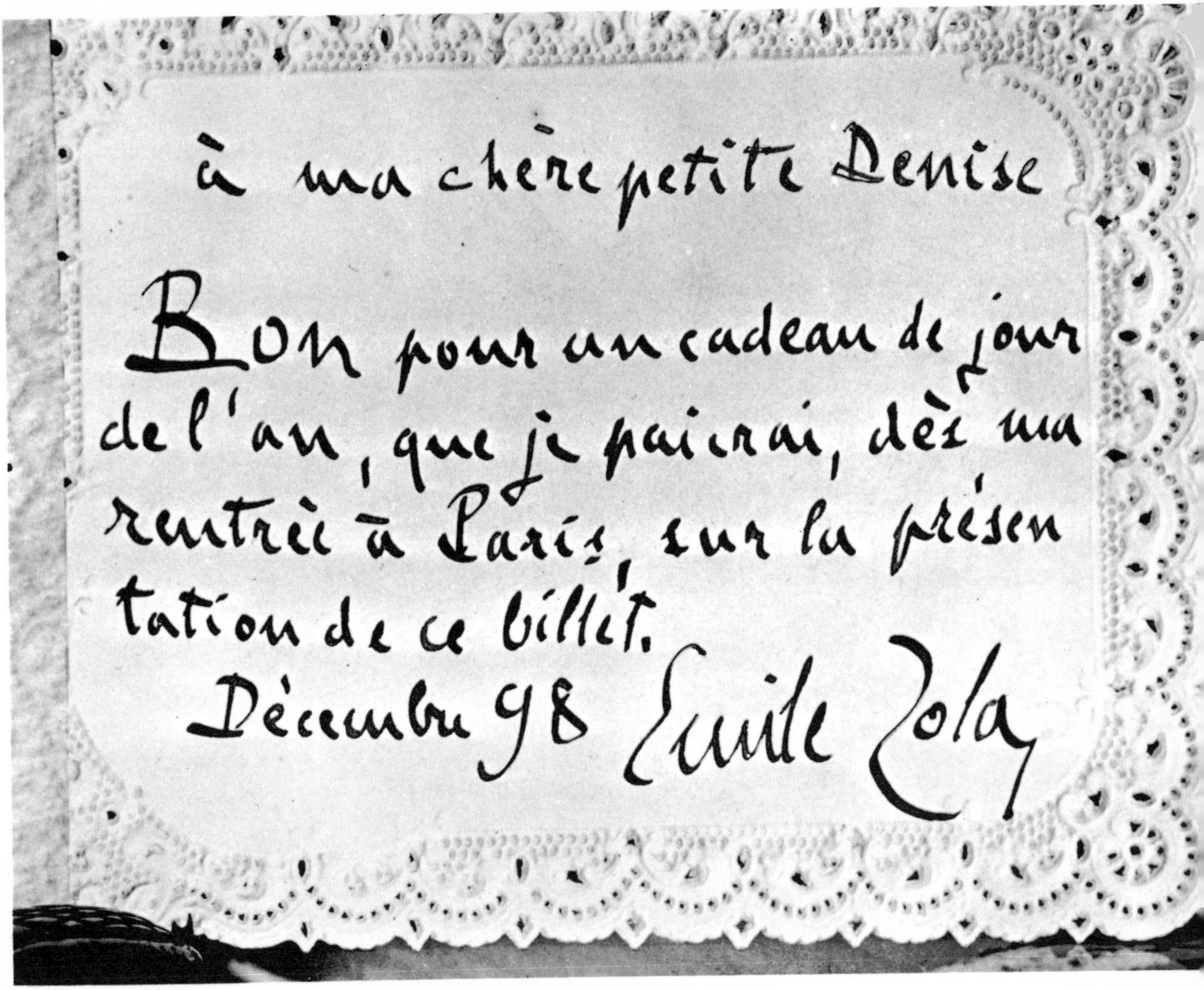

à ma chère petite Denise

Bon pour un cadeau de jour de l'an, que je paierai, dès ma rentrée à Paris, sur la présentation de ce billet.

Décembre 98 Emile Zola

Above: a note by Emile Zola. These words, which seem to have been hewn out of solid matter rather than written with a pen, are the work of a realist rather than a psychologist. The stroke is thick, the punctuation heavy; this, and the deliberate cross-strokes, are amply offset by the broad and sober motion of the signature.

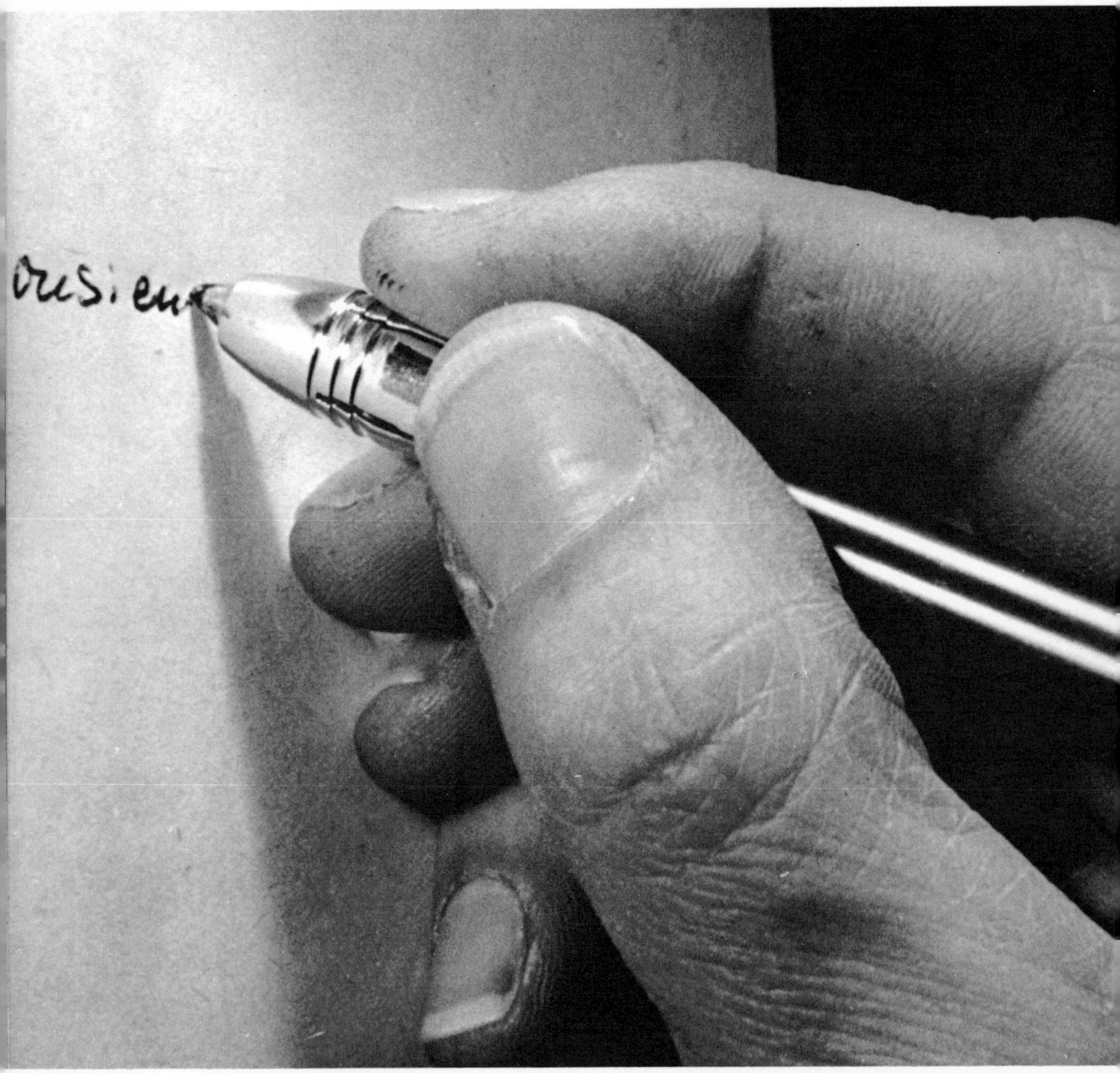

tion from neighboring signs, it will have only a relative meaning, as it may be attributable to a variety of physiological causes. Descending handwriting generally testifies to sadness; however, a short-lived anxiety, laziness, fear, lack of self-confidence, fatigue, sickness, or even an awkwardly placed sheet of writing paper can result in descending handwriting.

The main thing to look for is the *dominant signs*, which determine the value of accessory signs. Beginners are tempted to take short cuts in the graphological art by exaggerating the importance of minor signs; they may, for example, be fascinated by a single hook, or by the cross-stroke on a *t*, and neglect the general features of the hand altogether. The prime criterion for the assessment of a sign is its intensity value.

The *situation value* is the second element; by itself, an inward-turning hook at the beginning or end of a letter does not necessarily mean selfishness; it merely means that a person's thoughts are turned inwards, that he is concerned. The value of such a manifestation of the ego is to be assessed with reference to the handwriting as a whole.

Direction is an important value. "In mimicry, movements associated with pleasure and altruistic sentiments are expansive, centrifugal; movements of pain and selfish sentiments are concentric, centripetal, as if one were withdrawing from the world." Handwriting provides an application of this remark, since it necessarily involves moving in a great variety of directions; as is well known, the number of curves used in letter formation are equally divided between left- and right-turning. Experiments have shown that dynamogenic stimulation produces the movements depicted opposite: ↗↙.

By tracing the letters in the direction of the arrows, one produces a lively, active, sloping, well-disposed hand. Inhibitions and adverse stimuli, however, give the opposite effect: ↖↘. By tracing the letters in the direction of these last arrows, one arrives at an overturned, angular hand, with signs of personality, stiffness and tenacity. A distinction is drawn between right hands, which are evidence of activity, ardor, simplicity, virtue, and left hands, which are slower, sluggish, lacking in spontaneity and rich in signs of selfishness.

From the foregoing it is clear that, in order to interpret a sign properly, one has to form a general judgment about its author, and to decide, first of all, whether he is, generally speaking, a superior or an inferior person; this is followed by an examination to determine whether the qualities or defects noted relate to the mind, the will or to morality. These were the principles on which Crépieux-Jamin based his method of interpretation of signs. He established the relationships between handwriting and the character by associating graphological signs with psychological signs.

Handwriting by Nietzsche. 1889 (first specimen): the philosopher of the Will *of power and the* superman *was shortly to lose his reason. The broken head on the capitals is a harbinger of mental collapse. The stroke is still full and apparently firm. Yet the drive of the* ego *towards the* super-ego *is slackening. The determination to surpass himself was henceforth never to be more than a simple desire to exist. Two years later (second specimen), Nietzsche had gone mad.*

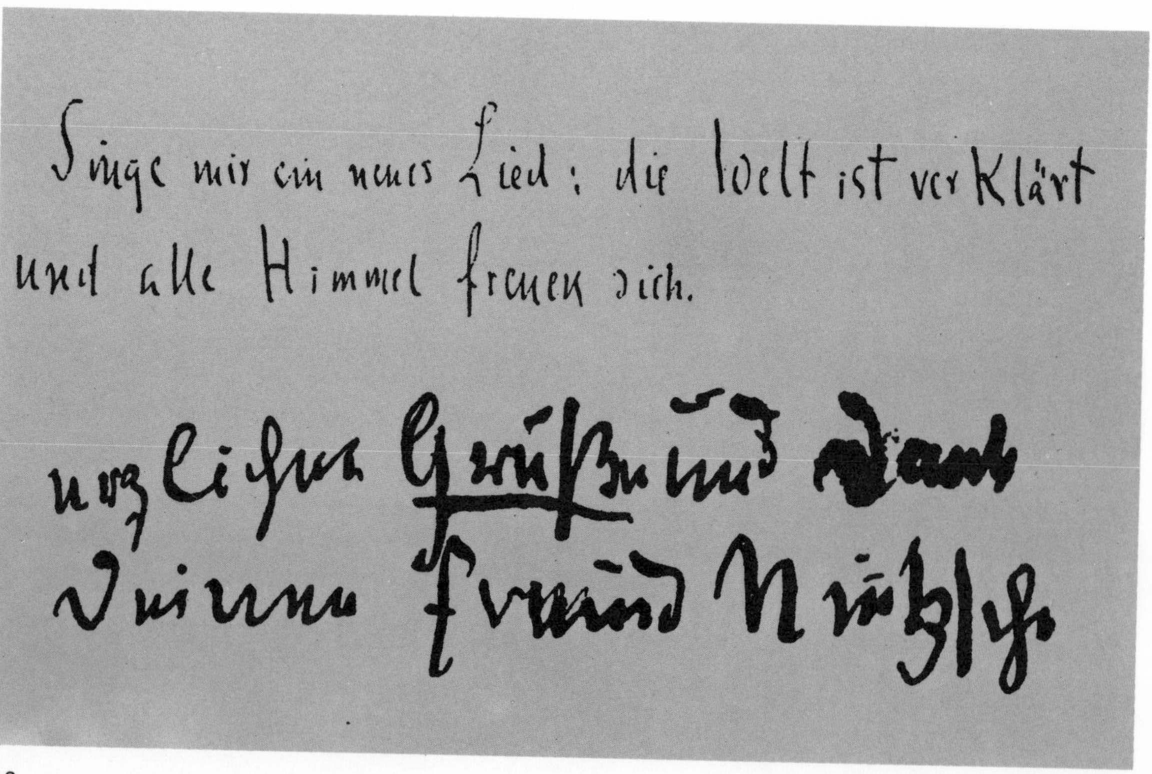

Graphography: a doctor "recording" a person's handwriting. On the following pages, the reader will find some interesting records produced by this device.

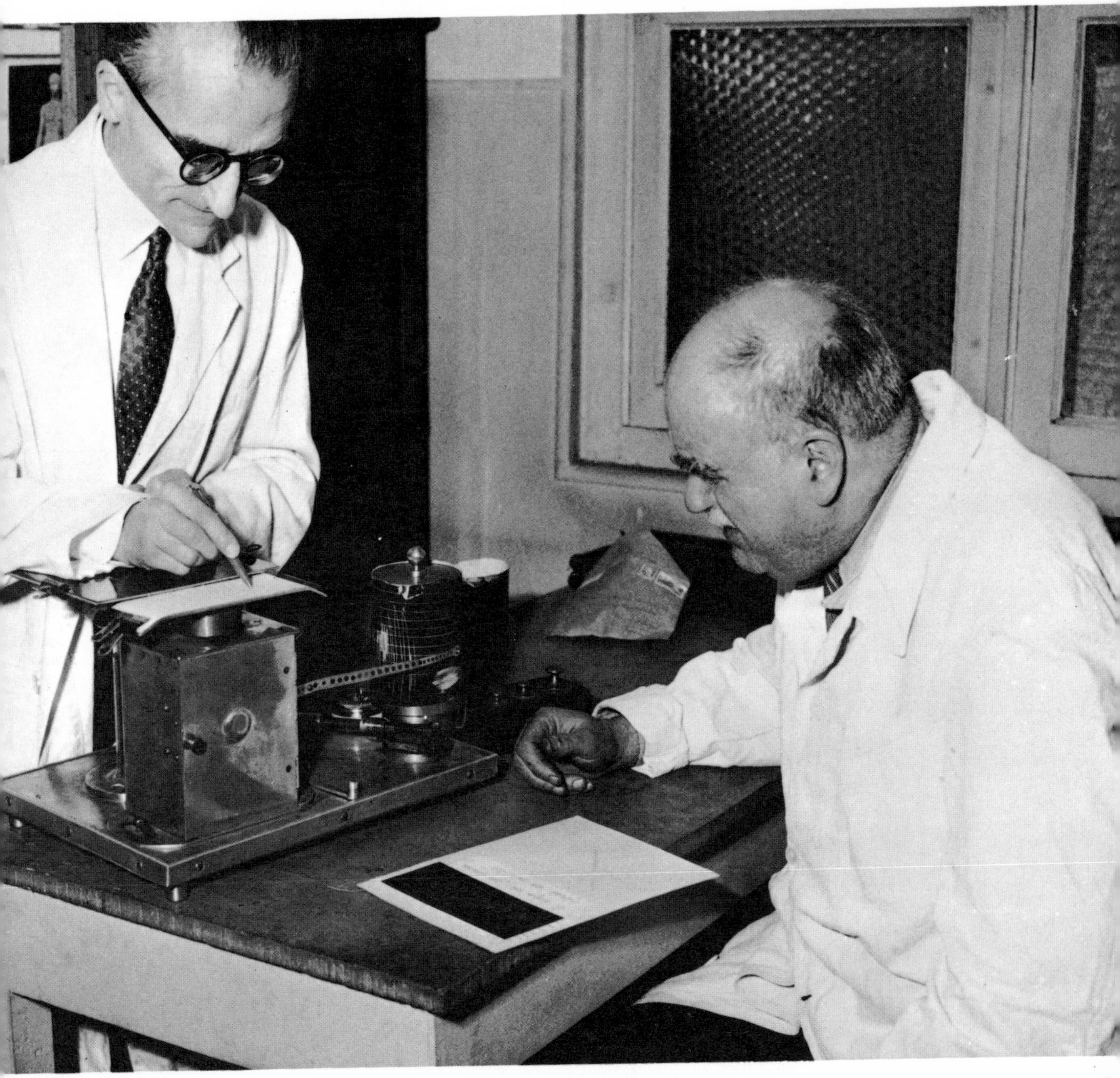

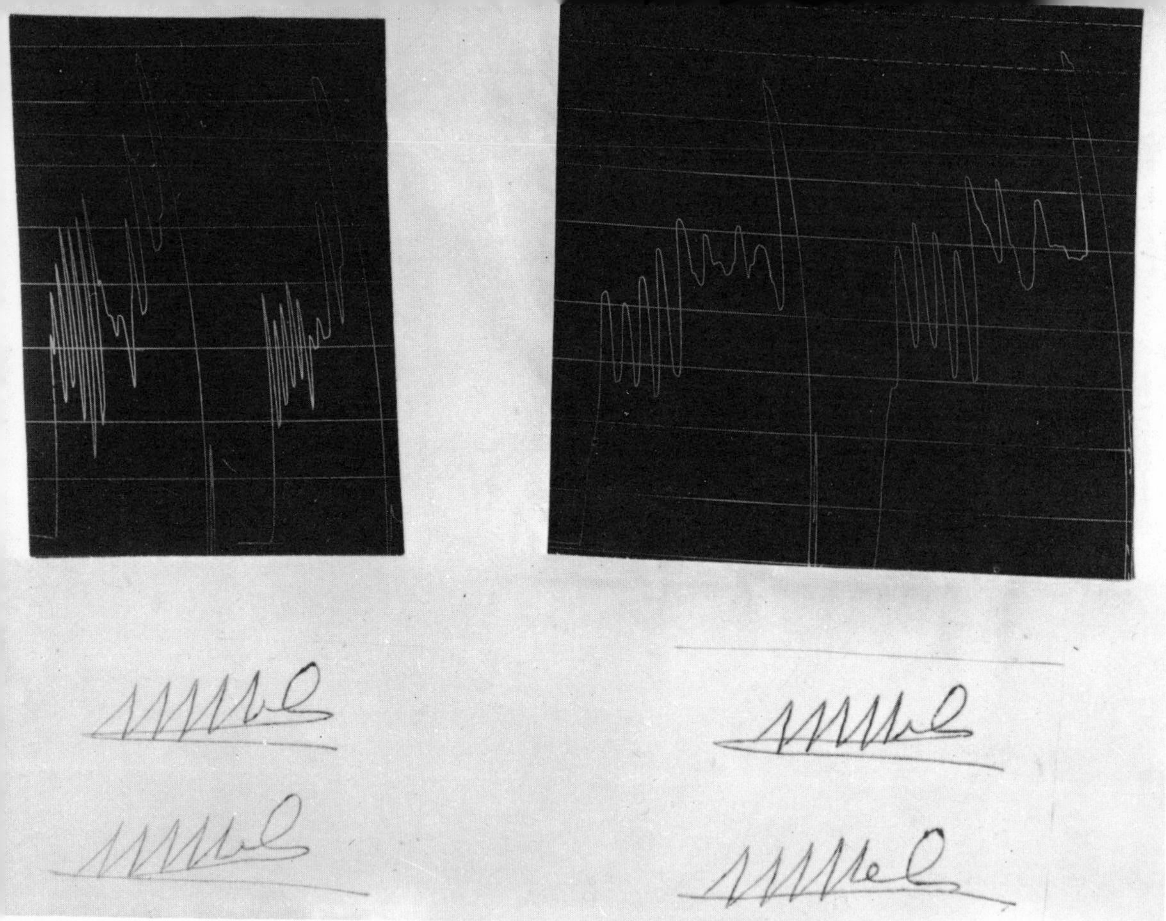

Above: left, two signatures by the same person; right, apparently identical signatures, the falseness of which is revealed by graphograms. Below the same words ("Nature"), written by two different people, with corresponding graphograms.

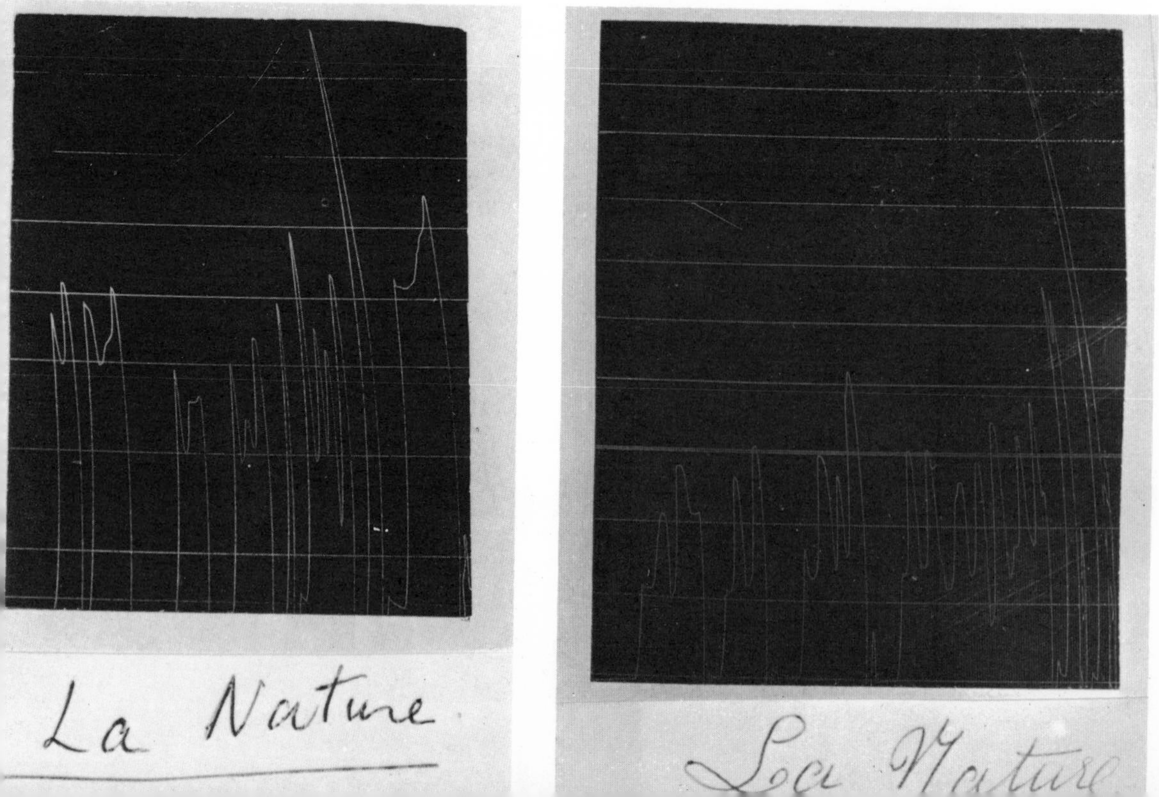

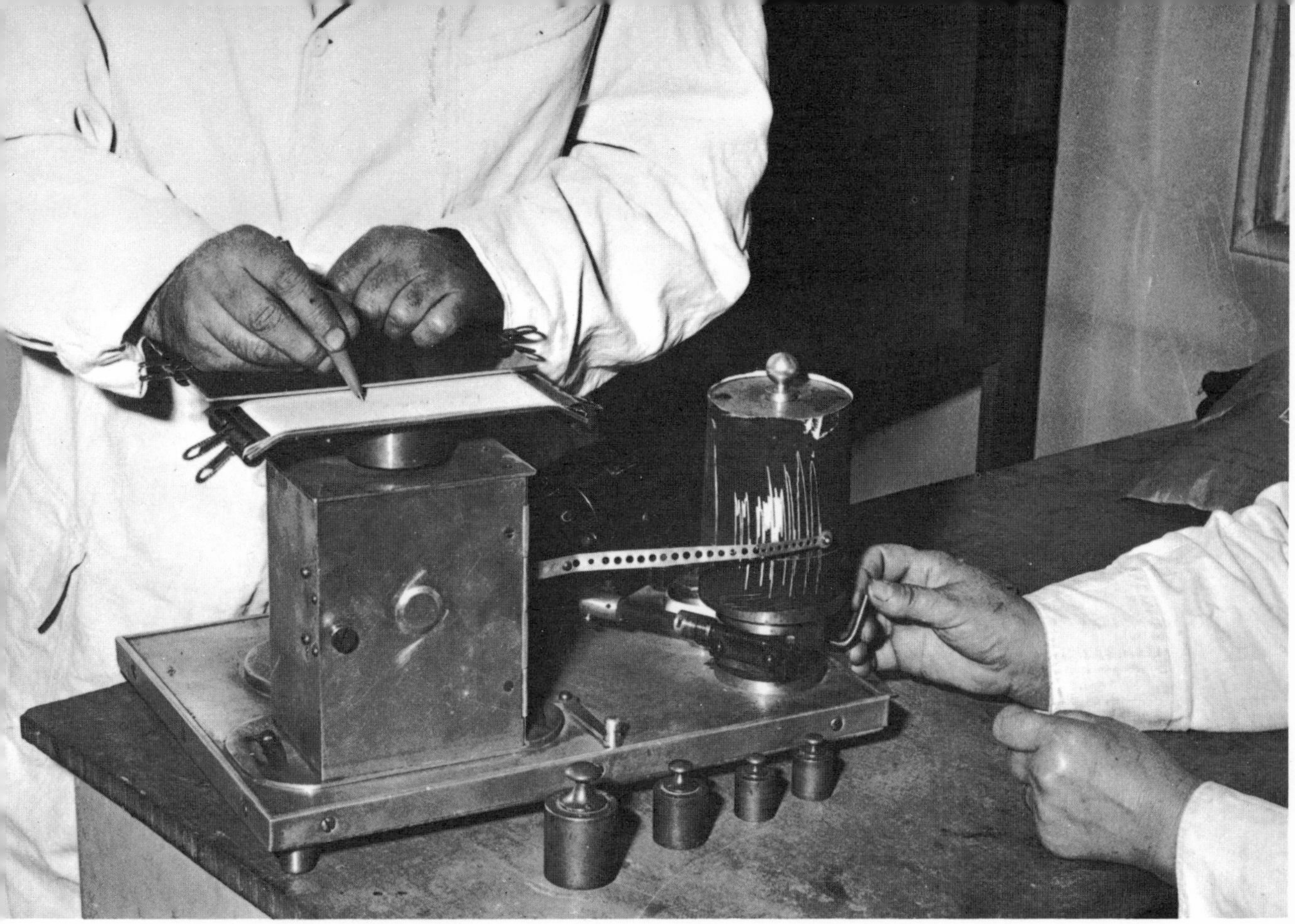

Handwriting graphogram in continuous printout. Even though graphography is not directly related to graphology, it confirms all our subject's findings.

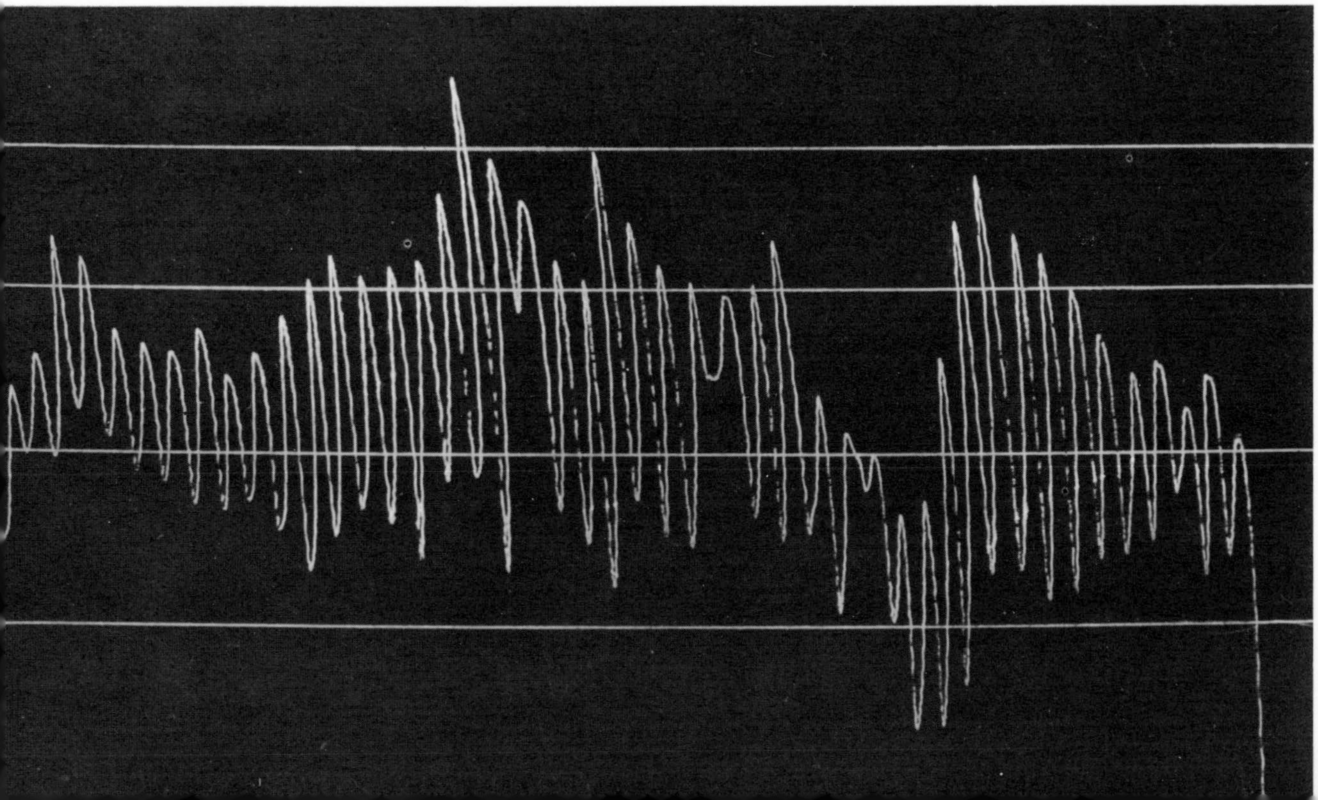

An injurious lie is an
uncommendable thing; there.

Mark Twain

1

Patriae inserviendo consumor.

2

v. Bismarck

Citoyen President

salut et fraternité

Fragonard

3

Emanuel Geibel

4

Une oeuvre d'art est un coin
de la nature

Emile Zola

5

4. The graphological examination.

Graphology consists of three parts: the study of general signs, the study particular signs, and the study of the resultants.

1. *General signs*. The general signs are noted during the examination of the hand as a whole, while one is examining the height, width, inclination, regularity, etc. They are not difficult to recognize and interpret. It is customary to attribute regular, calm handwriting to thoughtful, calm minds, odd handwriting to eccentrics, and blurred handwriting to untidy people, etc. As we have already seen, the general signs can lead to different interpretations according to the qualities of superiority or inferiority of the writer, and concomitant or accessory meanings. We shall give a definition of the general signs, with some examples, in order to illustrate the tables more fully. Although graphological signs are usually easy to understand, the reader might find a supplementary explanation useful.

An ascending handwriting is a hand in which the lines rise to right or to left (fig. 1).

In descending handwriting the lines descend from left to right.

Both these of these types of handwriting are dealt with in the next chapter.

Big handwriting; the letters are tall (fig. 2).

Small handwriting; the letters are small.

Angular handwriting; there are angles at the base of the letters (fig. 3).

Rounded handwriting; the curves are accentuated (fig. 4).

Sober handwriting; the lines, particularly the ends, are well contained. Restraint is shown in the movements of the pen (fig. 5).

Vigorous handwriting contains large strokes of the pen, either within the words, in the endings, or the in the signature.

Hesitant handwriting lacks precision in the formation of the lines, with an ill-determined direction and an irregular trembling motion (fig. 6).

Trembling handwriting differs from the preceding types in that the uncoordinated nervous movements persist.

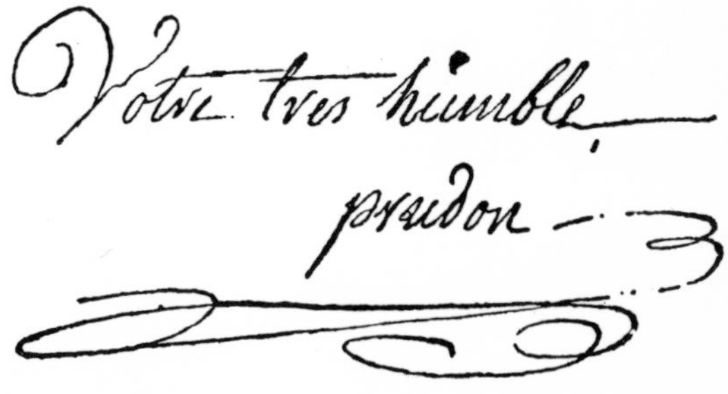

6

Ornate handwriting has flourishes, patterns and scrolls (fig. 7).

Simple handwriting has no scrolls.

Calligraphic, or *official*, handwriting was taught in the schools for many years. It is regular, unpretentious, legible, rounded, moderate and lacking in original character (fig. 8).

Even handwriting; words and letters are of equal height and inclination; lines always follow the same direction, which is invariable in autographs of the same author.

Uneven handwriting; uneven height, inclination, direction of the lines, or differing from one autograph to another.

Tidy handwriting, with an orderly arrangement of lines, margins and punctuation.

Unitidy handwriting shows no regard for margins, spaces between words and lines, nor the signs of handwriting (cross-strokes on *t*, and punctuation).

Clear handwriting, marked above all by spacing between the lines.

Confused handwriting; words and lines merge, capital letters encroach on neighboring lines, or lines are too close together.

Straight, stiff handwriting is strictly horizontal, and has no undulation at the base of the letters (fig. 9).

Serpentine handwriting goes up and down, within the same word or on the same line.

Vertical handwriting; the letters all stand upright.

Tilted handwriting; the letters all slope to the left (fig. 10).

Sloping handwriting; the letters all slope to the right.

Cramped handwriting; words or lines close together.

Spaced-out handwriting; the words are

7

8

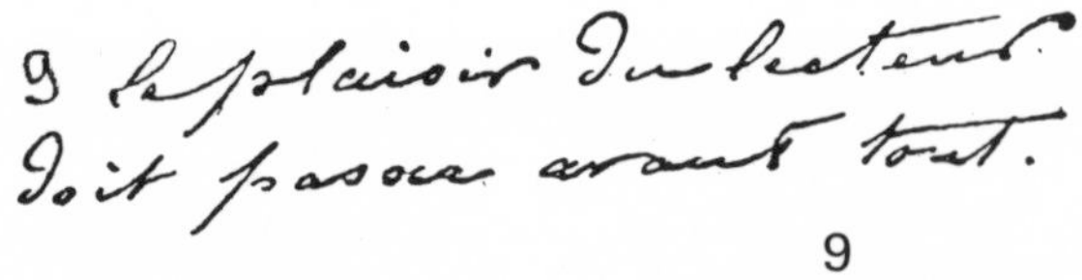

9

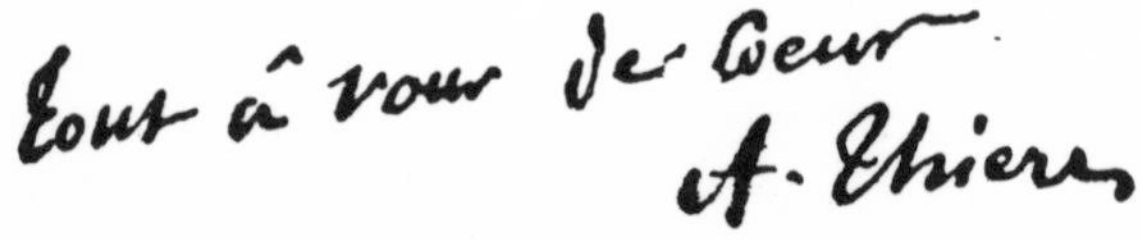

10

11

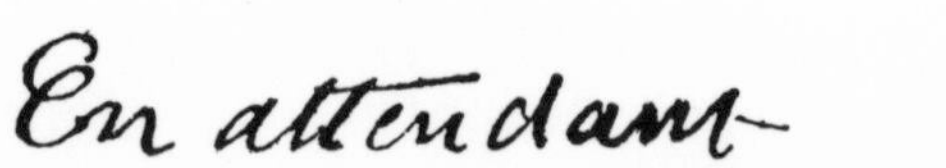

12

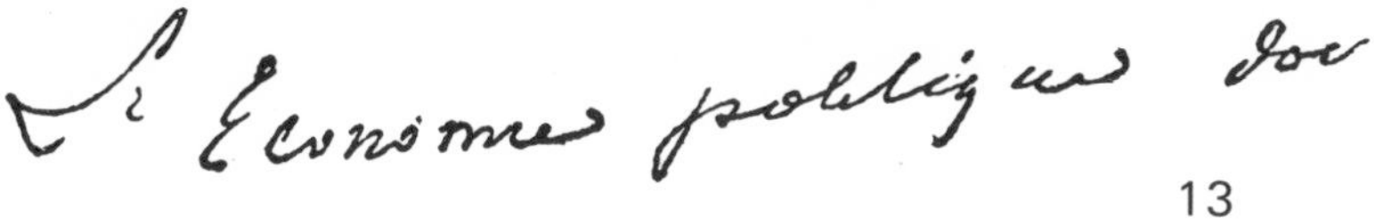

13

spaced far apart.

Odd handwriting; this style departs gratuitously from ordinary forms.

Light handwriting is fine and delicate.

Heavy handwriting is thick, with heavy pressure on the pen (fig. 11).

Clean handwriting has precise contours.

Agitated handwriting is a variant on irregular handwriting: the mobility and feeling of stimulation are more pronounced.

Complex handwriting contains more strokes of the pen than are necessary for the formation of the letters.

Simplified handwriting contains less strokes of the pen than are necessary for the regular formation of the letters.

Corrected handwriting; in order to make his writing more easily legible, the writer goes over it a second time an adds corrections where necessary.

Slow handwriting (fig. 12).

Fast handwriting (fig. 13).

Handwriting *varying in size* according to the format of the paper used. If the paper is big, the handwriting is big also, and vice versa. Thus, when writing postcards, some people reduce the size of their normal hand, whereas others shorten their message, rather than altering their style, or simply write across what they have already written. On pages 34 to 37, the reader will find a detailed table of the General Signs, with their meaning.

2. *Particular signs*. These signs are harder to find than the general signs; they are provided by words, letters, endings, punctuation, signature flourishes, etc. Much patient research was needed before it was discovered that an *n* replaced by a *u* means kindness, that

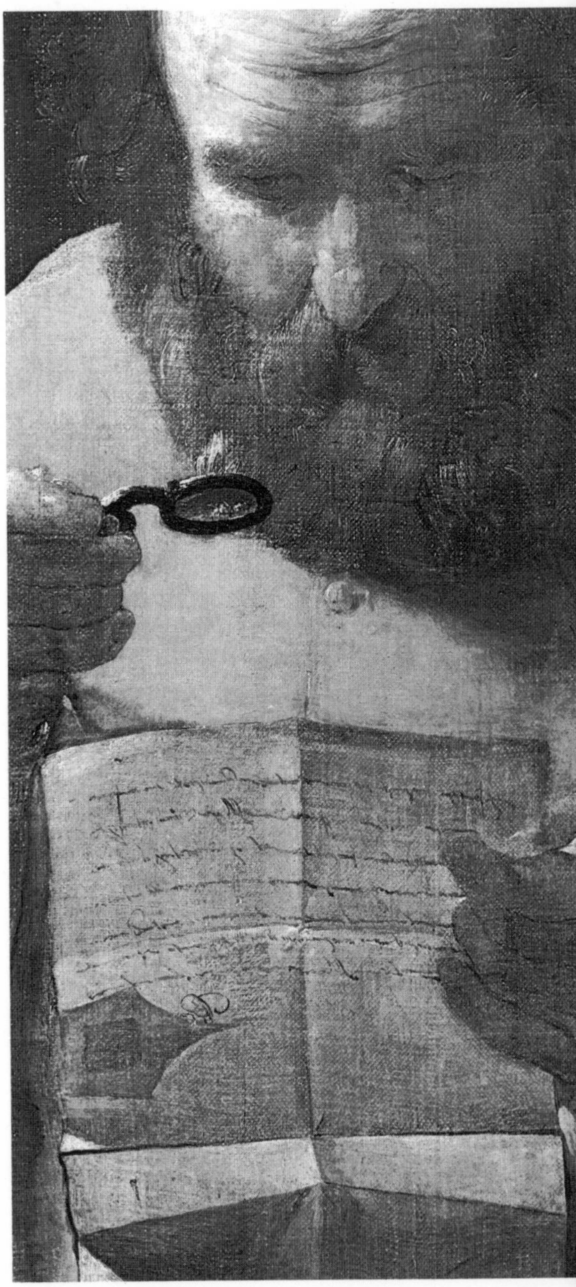

very low capital letters are a sign of hypocrisy or introspection, or that excessively large capitals are a sign of imagination. Unlike the general signs, the particular signs do not seem to lend themselves to accessory meanings; being specialized graphologically, they seem also to reflect certain particular traits of character as a consequence. However, it is possible to find concomitant meanings through them. Spindle-shaped words, with barely completed endings, thus signify impenetrability; sophistication and distrust and even hypocrisy are often concomitant with impenetrability; spindle-shaped words can also signify haste: the writer is in such a hurry that he is content merely to express his thoughts, without bothering to finish his words. A simple horizontal line reflects reason, loyalty, justice, love of clarity, order or distrust, and this same trait can at the same time indicate that the writer is lively, energetic, brutal. However, it is usually fairly easy to find the true significance of a sign by reference to neighboring signs. The intensity and the frequency of a sign strongly suggest the concomitant qualities associated with it. Conversely, relatively slight incidence of such signs, especially if they are weakly written, makes it less likely that the person in question has these qualities. In any case, the character viewed as a whole will always guide us in the appreciation of the signs.

Let us define some of the particular signs. There is no need to define all of them, since, in most cases, an indication is usually tantamount to a definition.

Words ending *in a point* are sometimes known as *sword-shaped*, as they resemble the tip of a sword. Letters are bigger at the beginning of the word than at the end (fig. 14).

Swelling words have their first few letters smaller than the rest.

Spindle-shaped words are legible only for their first half; the end of the word is made up of a single line, more or less long and sinuous (fig. 15).

Juxtaposed letters are placed side by side but not joined.

Later on in this work, the reader will find a detailed table of the particular signs with their significance.

3. *Resultants.* "The term *resultant* is used to describe the product of various signs. For example, the letter *t* with a weak cross-stroke denotes weakness of will, whereas broad sweeps of the pen are a sign of great imagination. They are two signs. Handwriting which contains both of them belongs, without a doubt, to a coward, since lack of will-power is a prime factor causing that condition, and it is further compounded by his imagination, which vastly exaggerates any dangers which

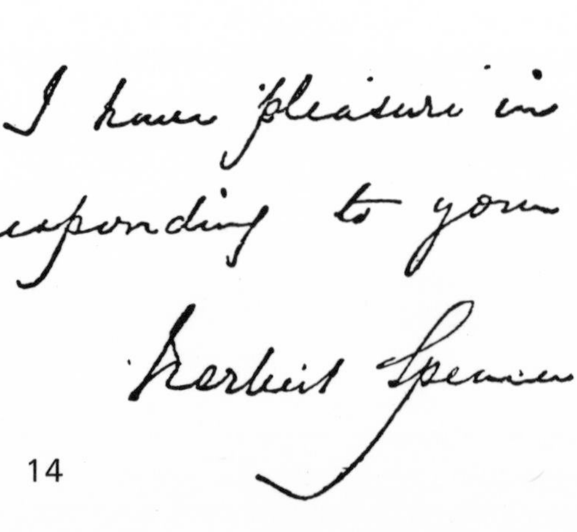

14

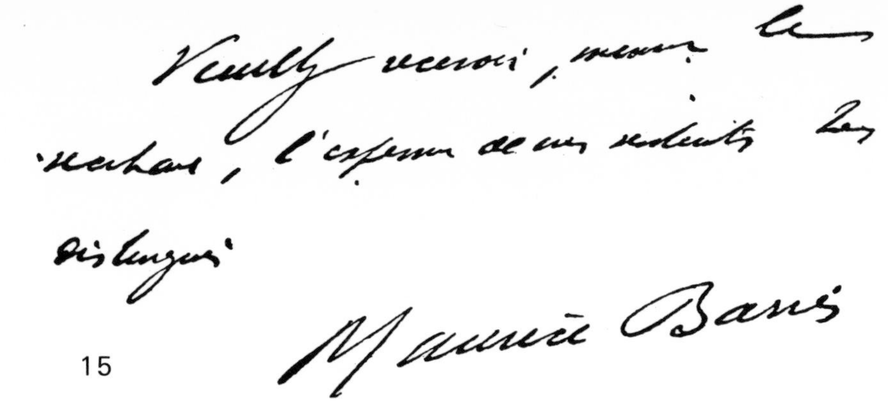

15

he may be facing. Cowardice is a resultant." (Crépieux-Jamin).

This example well illustrates the role the resultants play in graphology; however, this role becomes possible only if the resultants can be determined with some certainty, since it involves, above all, a full reconstitution of the intellectual and moral personality of a person "harmonizing the product of all the signs which make up his handwriting". In other words, these signs must be interpreted not merely individually, but from the point of view of their inter-relations. Here we enter into the truly philosophical side of the subject. The link which exists between a character trait and a certain handwriting feature is not, of itself, enough; it is essential that there should be laws for the composition of character emanating from the more general laws of psychology; without these laws, it is impossible to judge the relative importance of a sign, or to identify which out of a multitude of possible combinations of signs is really involved in a given case.

The resultants may be of various sorts. For example, two different signs for sophistication may be added together, and give a high degree of sophistication.

Sword-shaped words	... sophistication	great sophistication
Small handwriting	... sophistication	

This is a resultant based on *intensity*. Suppose we were to find the sign for sophistication allied to the sign for flexibility of mind; we would thereby obtain a new character trait – diplomacy. This would be a resultant based on *combination*.

Sword-shaped words	... sophistication	diplomacy
Serpentine handwriting	... flexibility of mind	

The greatest number of traits of character can combine in this way to produce resultants, thus leading the observer to certain complex elements of the personality which are reflected, not by a single sign, but by a comination of two or more signs, themselves representing as many elementary states of mind. For example, people who are quick to take offense have a mixture of pride and great sensitivity; vanity comes from pride in conjunction with vulgarity; cruelty comes from the threefold association of mediocre intelligence, a total lack of sensitivity and a powerful will; a strong temper is compatible with gentleness when it is accompanied by an authoritarian will and a lively imagination; a fondness for theft results from a combination of selfishness and hypocrisy, etc. A knowledge of resultants, through a study of their associated signs, is one of the most interesting aspects of graphology; it shows how such a study, which may have been started out of idle curiosity about a certain individual, can, if entrusted to a careful, skilled psychologist, reveal some very fundamental, but little known personality traits.

Even if graphology served only as a way of arriving at knowledge of the character, it would more than justify its existence; yet it also helps us, in its own special way, to discover the laws of the composition of the character, the most frequent psychic coincidences and combinations; it is an exceedingly valuable tool for psychological analysis.

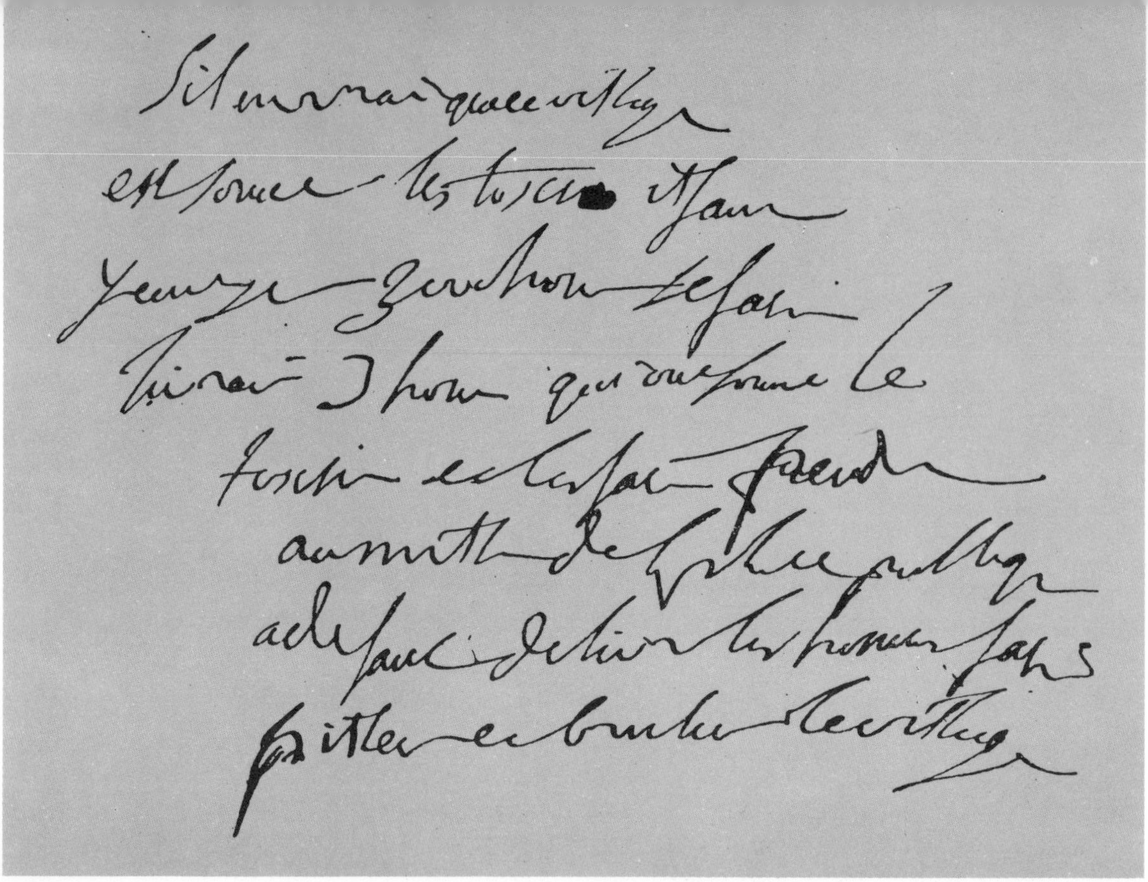

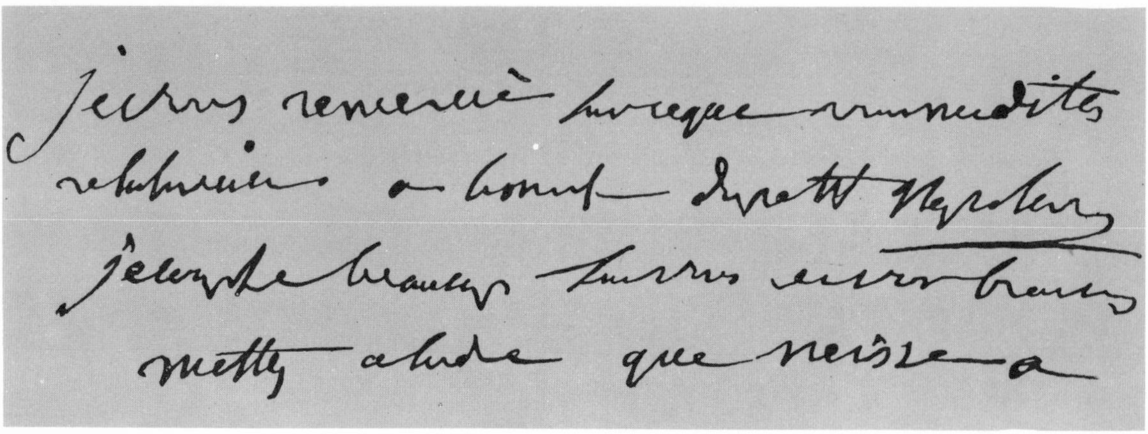

Two specimens of the handwriting of Napoleon: this style is striking on account of the intense motion which constantly drives it forward. Decisions and actions proceed apace, unencumbered by thought or caution. Under what appears to be disorder and agitation, it is possible to discern the unifying theme of intuition and instinct which, more than reason, account for Napoleon's genius, and led him from victories to disasters.
The first specimen is an order to capture the men of an enemy village who, at the approach of the Imperial army, had sounded the alarm. They were to be hung. It is followed by this sentence: "If the men cannot be captured, then sack and burn the village". A distinct relationship will be noticed between the nature of the message and the graphic style of the hand in which it was written.

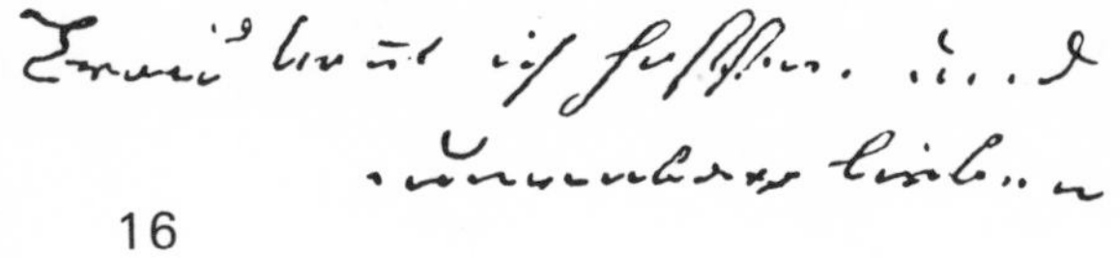

16

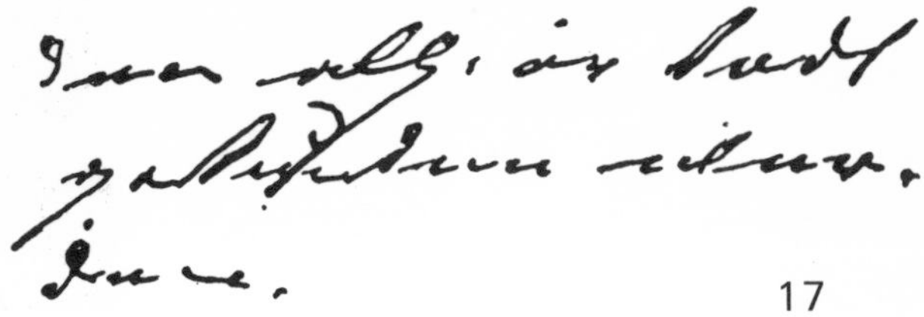

17

5. Rising and falling styles of handwriting.

Instinctively rising handwriting is a sign of success, prosperity, or, at least, ambition to achieve great things or acquire renown (see fig. 1).

Falling handwriting always signifies some kind of stroke of bad luck, a major obstacle to overcome in one's life, or a profound melancholy.

One author has referred, though without providing full explanations, to the strange fact that Napoleon's signatures rose or fell with his fortune. He also gave two specimens of this kind of hand; one of the writers had written his own epitaph, to be engraved on his tomb (fig. 16).

The second autograph is the work of a man about to commit suicide, and is his goodbye to the world (fig. 17).

But it is Napoleon's rising and falling signatures which make a truly rewarding study, as they follow remarkably closely the violent swings of fortune during his career.

The first is from 1793 (fig. 18).

In a letter addressed to the government, Captain Bonaparte, wishing to accompany his sister back home, claimed the mileage allowance provided for by the law. As can be seen, the Captain was not yet the favorite of fortune; his writing has an ambitious rise in it, yet, when he starts talking about domestic details, such as the number of cents per mile, it levels off a bit!

However, his signature rises unmistakably: it already has the strength and firmness of an energetic, persevering type; the final flourish seems to have been written with an iron bar!

The second signature is that of *General* Bonaparte, and is addressed to the Headquarters in Berlin (date: 13 Fructidor, year IV) of the French army. He merely signs a double *B*, with the very heavy final flourish which is an undisputed sign of stubbornness, perseverance and audacity (fig. 19).

The energetic flourish rises, as a sign of firmness, perseverance and ambition, and is, in every sense, the kind of handwriting one would expect from General Bonaparte.

18

19

1804.

20

1805.

21

1806.

22

1812, 21 septembre.

23

1812, 6 octobre.

24

Next comes the signature of Bonaparte, when Emperor in 1804 (fig. 20).

The graphologist referred to above begins his study of Napoleon's signatures at this point; we shall add some comments of our own.

1804

"Signature of Napoleon the Emperor. Outer dignity. Pageantry and homage. The Emperor crowned."

In this signature, remarkable above all for its energy, the man's soul, carried away by pride and a barely contained upsurge of joy, has revealed itself fully.

1805

"A signature taken from the end of a proclamation, after the battle of Austerlitz, 2 December 1805. The proud conqueror throws his head back, and sets off to scale Mount Bergauf (Bergan)."

This is a spontaneous explosion of victorious joy; the final flourish of the signature is like a hat tossed triumphantly into the air! (fig. 21).

1806

"Signature after the 1806 campaign. Hasty, laconic, almost Spartan."

The signature still has an iron-like quality about it, the N is firm, and the signature ends in a big and heavily accentuated period. It is as if he were placing a seal on his power (fig. 22).

1812, 21 September.

"The entry into a burning Moscow. Written in the glare of the fire during the retreat from Russia. Still bold, but concerned."

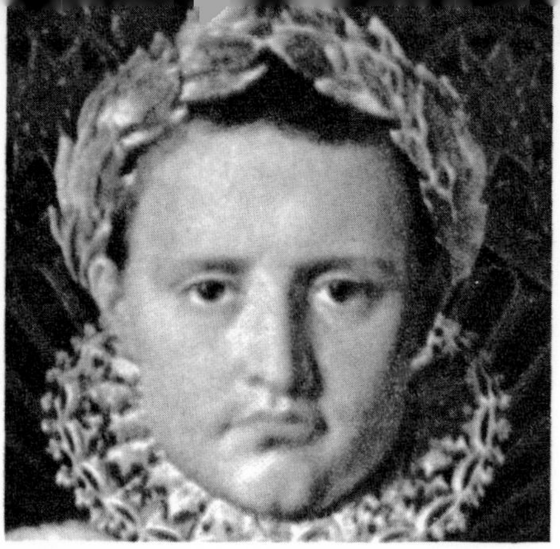

He is being abandoned by fortune. For the first time, his rising signature descends and then struggles to rise again. Here we are witnessing a spirit of defiance, rather than his previous ebullience (fig. 23).

1812, 6 October.

"On the retreat from Russia. Still bold, but now thoughtful as well."

The signature falls, and then recovers its rising line (fig. 24).

1813

"Signature on a document which he signed at Erfurt, 23 October 1813, after the loss of the battle of Leipzig. A brooding dissatisfaction" (fig. 25).

This is a big, desperate, sprawling signature. It hurtles downwards, and then rises again menacingly; yet its line becomes thinner, while an ink blot falls from his pen and fortuitously drives his signature even lower.

1814

"4 April, 1814. Little noise."

A descending, but nonetheless excitable *N*. This could be the signature of a man rushing towards a precipice (fig. 26).

Signature on Saint-Hélène.

"The signature on Saint-Hélène is descending, sad, broken and crushed by grief" (fig. 27).

Half of his name swoops downwards, even lower than before, never to rise again. Yet, the final line is still an emphatic gesture of stubborn resistance. He is resigned, as it is all over for him, but posterity will not forget his dynamic, turbulent life, and will doubtless set matters right.

1813.

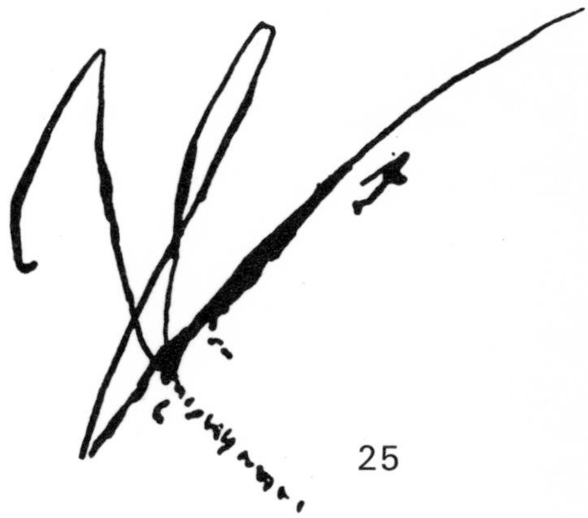

25

1814, Fontainebleau.

26

Signature à Sainte-Hélène.

27

28

Albert, Count of Wallenstein.

It will be noticed that Napoleon, like all great men, was highly sensitive. The signatures follow and reflect the various phases of his destiny.

He himself admitted that he was a man much given to intuitive feelings about the future; to some extent, these feelings must have radiated outwards and been perceived by those around him.

The author failed to point out that Wallenstein's signature, like that of Napoleon on St. Helena, dips sharply downwards; moreover, the signatures of the two men are strikingly similar in form, and firmness, besides the fact that both of them serve as forecasts of the future (fig. 28). A reader familiar with German literature must certainly know Wallenstein, through Schiller's brilliant trilogy.

Everyone knows that Albrecht, Count of Friedland, born on 14 September, 1593, was assassinated on 25 February 1634 (on the orders of the Emperor, who was increasingly distressed at the growth in his power), after a career in which his military abilities had taken him to the level of Count of the Empire, Prince of the Empire, Duke of Friedland, Sagan, Magdeburg, and General of the Baltic Sea and the Ocean. Here we have reproduced the signature of the famous Wallenstein.

This exaggerated signature indicates a frank, loyal man—chivalrous, perhaps proud, and most certainly a man who set out with great ambitions; melancholy rather than excitable, but doomed to a tragic end.

Despite Schiller's attempt to rehabilitate the hero of his tragedy, it was excessive ambition that led to his downfall; here again, we have evidence of a moral collapse.

My best wishes

29

30

31

32

33

34

35

36

37

38

39

40

41

42

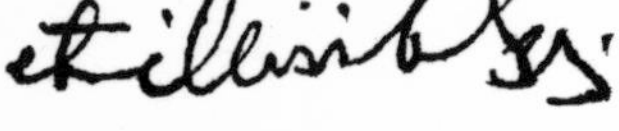

43

44

45

46

GRAPHIC SIGNS

Handwriting
big (29) . . . .

small (30) . . . .
angular (31) . . . .
rounded (32) . . . .

sober (33) . . . .

lively (34) . . . .

hesitant (35) . . . .
trembling (36) . . . . . .

ornate (37) . . . .

simple (38) . . . .
calligraphic (39) . . . .
even (40) . . . .
uneven (41) . . . .

tidy (42) . . . .

untidy (43) . . . .

clear (44) . . . .
confused (45) . . . .
straight and rigid (46)

6. The general signs.

ARY MEANINGS	MEANINGS more specifically relating to *general superiority*	*general inferiority*	CONCOMITANT RELATIONSHIPS *Accessory meanings*
spirations	Pride	Slow thinking	Generosity, aristocratic pride, long-sightedness, imagination.
ness	Fineness	Meanness	Narrow-mindedness.
ornness	Firmness	Hardness	Selfishness, positive mind.
eness	Gracefulness	Weak will	Imagination, softness, aesthetic sense, laziness, cowardice.
ration, ghtfulness	Prudence	Distrust	Reserve, clarity, judgment, modesty, economy, hypocrisy, dignity, modesty.
ination	Imagination	Mental agitation	Gaiety, grace, silliness, stupidity, pride, fondness for gossip.
ation	Indecision	Hesitation	Fear, shyness, embarrassment.
ge	Old age	Old age.	Fatigue, excitement, alcoholism, cold, fright, indignation, anger.
tched	Grace or pretentiousness	Commonplace fatuousness	Vanity, coquettishness, aesthetic sense, insignificance, meanness.
icity	Modesty	Insignificance	Loyalty
quacy	Posture	Insignificance	Love of the conventional; narrow mind.
tancy	Logic	Equanimity	Firmness, exactness, calm.
tivity	Mental flexibility	Versatility	Eclecticism, capriciousness, unsteady character given to fantasy, agitation.
	Order in one's ideas	Material order	Sense of order, attention to minute detail.
der	Lack of material order	Disorder in the mind	Carelessness, no attention to accuracy.
y	Clear thinking	Clear mind	Love of order.
usion	Lack of clarity	Confused mind	Disorder, madness.
ess	Firm mind	Firmness	Inflexibility, spirit of routine, severity.

47

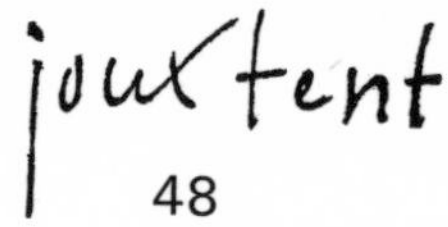

48

49

50

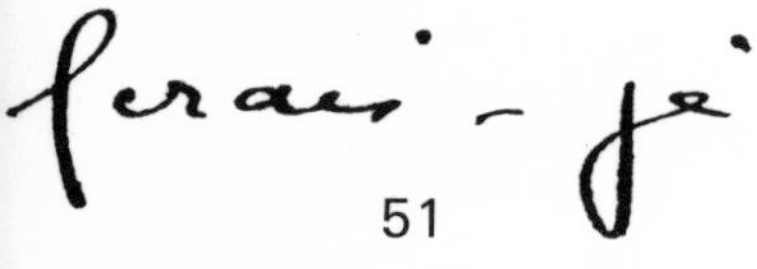

51

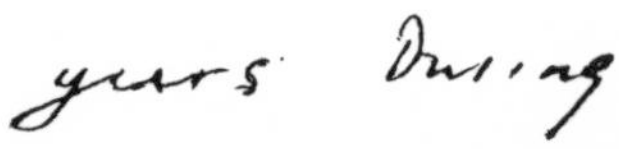

52

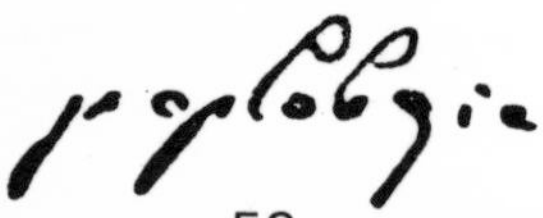

53

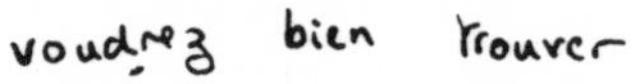

54

55

56

57

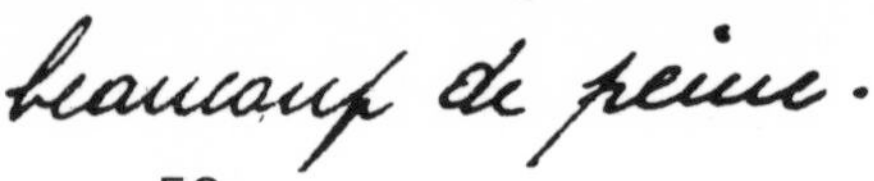

58

59

serpentine (47) . . . .

vertical (48) . . . .
backward leaning (4
sloping (50) . . . .

cramped . . . .
spaced out (51) . . . .
odd . . . .
light (52) . . . .
thick (53) . . . .
clean (54) . . . .
agitated (55) . . . . . .

complicated . . . . . .

simplified (56) . . . .
retouched (57) . . . .

slow (58) . . . .
fast (59) . . . .
changing . . . .
of varying size . . . .

NARY MEANINGS	MEANINGS *more specifically relating to* — *general superiority*	*general inferiority*	CONCOMITANT RELATIONSHIPS *Accessory meanings*
al flexibility	Fineness	Lies	Diplomacy, tact, agitation, contrariness, easily impressionable character, eye disorders.
ensitivity	Reason	Poor sensitivity	Energy, coldness, selfishness.
st	Distrust	Distrust	Restrained sensitivity, dissimulation.
tivity	Sensibility	Sensibility	Passion, touchiness, personality disorders, desire for approval, affection.
mony	Economy	Stinginess	Reserve,
gality	Generosity	Disorder	Love of comfort.
haracter	Originality	Madness	Caprices.
acy	Delicate mind	Weakness	Ill-adjusted personality, sensitivity.
ality	Sensuality	Bestiality	Dull, commonplace mind, gluttony.
ated mind	Cultivated mind	Cultivated mind	Preciseness of thought, clarity.
usness	Stimulation	Exaltation	Fatigue, fear, alcoholic stimulation, anger.
f preciseness	Lack of preciseness	Lack of preciseness	Sign of madness, bad faith.
seness	Culture	Culture	Loyalty, ability, simplicity.
t for rfection	Quest for perfection	Quest for perfection	Return to the first movement.
mind	Timidity, calm	Slow thinking	Softness.
ty	Keen mind	Vivacity	Ardor.
lity	Flexibility of mind	Cheating	Versatility, caprice.
bility of mind.	Flexibility of mind	Flexibility of mind.	Good taste, intelligence.

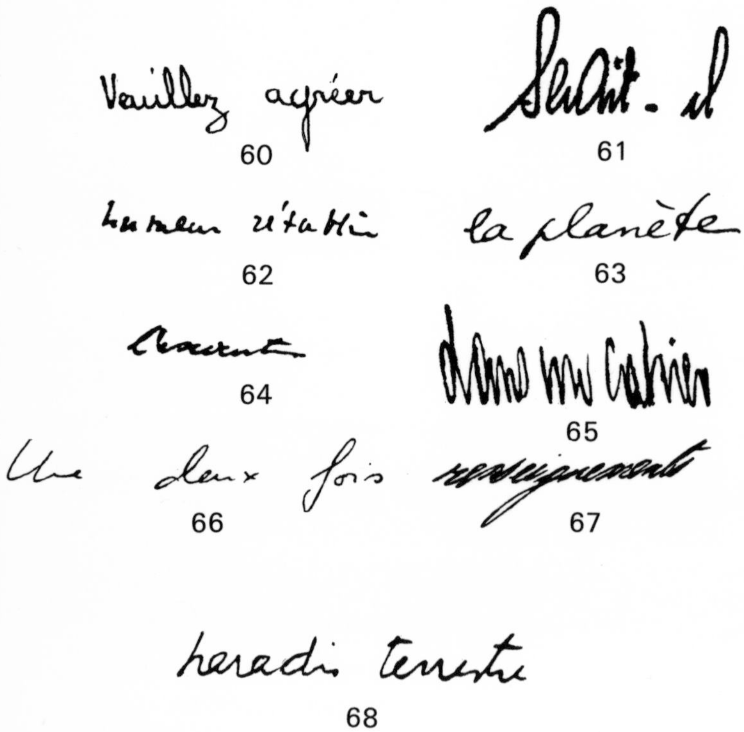

Graphic signs

Words in which the letters are of un… height (60) . . . . .
with uneven letters

ending in a point (6…
becoming larger (6…
omitted . . . .
with tapering, illegi… final letters (64) .
emphasis provided by increasing height . . . .

cramped together (65) . . . .
spaced out (66) . . .
with spaced out letters . . . .

with cramped letters (67) . . . . .
Letters connect (68

connected in group… of 3 or 4 (69) . . .

7. The special signs.

DINARY MEANINGS	MEANINGS more specifically relating to general superiority	general inferiority	CONCOMITANT RELATIONSHIPS Accessory meanings
titude	Rectitude	Rectitude	Justice, calm judgment, moderation.
xibility f mind.	Indecisiveness	Hesitation, weakness, lies.	
tlety of mind	Subtlety of mind	Shrewdness	Lying.
veness	Candor	Credulity	Loyalty, simplicity.
ughtlessness	Absent-mindedness	Flippancy	Carelessness,
enetrability	Craftiness	Dissimulation	Distrust, hypocrisy, rash behaviour.
ltation			
simony	Economy	Stinginess	Stinginess, reserve.
digality	Generosity	Disorder	Fondness for comfort.
y to talk to	Kindness	Easy to get on with	Generosity, fondness for comfort.
leasant haracter	Hardness of heart	Unpleasant character	Reserve, economy.
ctical mind. easoning owers	Logic, order in one's ideas	False reasoning	Nonentity.
imilation	Assimilation and comparison	Assimilation	Eclecticism, encyclopedic spirit.

69

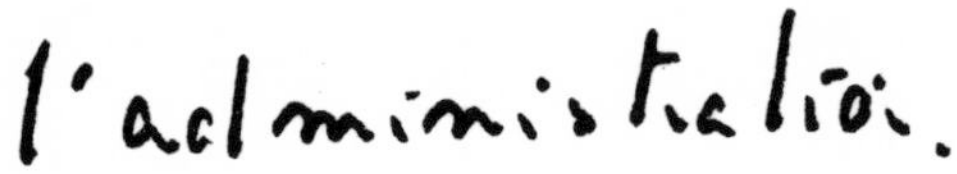

70

71

72

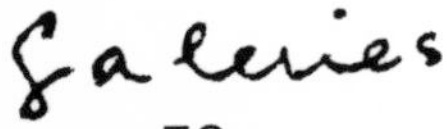

73

74

75

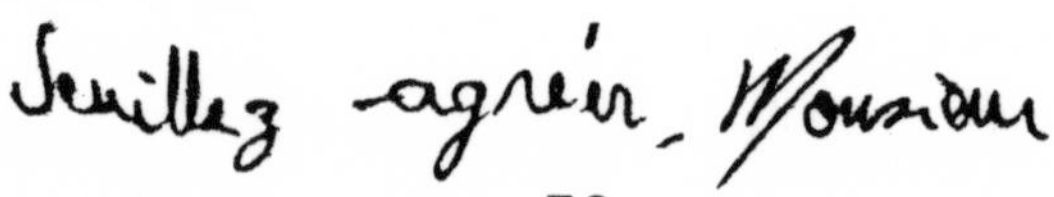

76

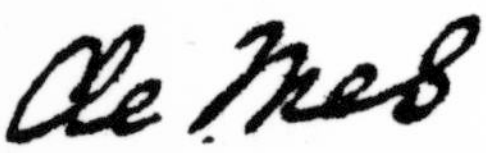

77

not connected, placed side by side (70) . . . .
open at the top (*o, a,* etc.) (71) . . .
normally closed (72)
open beneath (*o, a,* etc.) (73)
typographic shape (74)
commonplace shape as in handwriting models . . . .
thick, or with downstrokes swollen . .
in the middle (75) . . .
alternating between sloping and straight (76) . . . . .
starting with a hock . . . .
starting with a fast, rounded stroke . . . .
starting with a sharp, straight stroke . . .
small letters (usually *a,r,s)* bigger than the others (77) . . . . . .
ending in a club . . . .
ending uncertainly . .
ending, but not in a club . . . .
shafts instead of loops (78) . . . .

INARY MEANINGS	MEANINGS *more specifically relating to* *general superiority*	*general inferiority*	CONCOMITANT RELATIONSHIPS *Accessory meanings*
llectual feeling	Theory, creation, intuition	Utopia	Systematic mind, paradox.
nness of mind	Frankness	Casual attitude	Effusiveness.
riety	Discretion	Propriety	Reserve.
imulation	Dissimulation	Hypocrisy	Lying.
d taste	Art	Art	Culture, distinction.
r taste	Lack of good taste	Commonplace mind	Crudeness.
entity	Lack of originality	Nonentity	Passive mind.
suality	Sensuality	Base sensuality	Gluttony.
le	Fickleness of sentiment	Caprice	Excitement.
uisitive instinct			Selfishness.
ety			Good humour.
trariness.	Contrariness	Quibbling	
gination, xaltation.		Violence	Madness (?).
rmination cisiveness	Determination		
tained energy	Prudence		Order, economy.
ivated mind			Simplification, clarity, tidiness.

78

79

80

81

82

83

GRAPHIC SIGNS

with swollen loops
loops (79) . . . . . .
tall capital letters
(80) . . . .

medium-sized
capitals . . . .
low capitals . . . .
capitals joined to
the next letter (81)
capitals joined to
the next letter
after a
loop (82) . . . .
capitals instead
of small letters . . .
capitals replaced
by small letters . . .
capitals where they
belong . . . .
capital raised by
the base (83) . . . . .
Stroke, between
phrases . . . .
at the end of a line,
to fill out the line
(84). . . . .
straight, horizontal
stroke (generally) .
undulating
(in general) . . . . . .
Punctuation, careless
careful punctuation .

Dots, changed into
accents (85) . . . . .

INARY MEANINGS	MEANINGS more specifically relating to: *general superiority*	MEANINGS more specifically relating to: *general inferiority*	CONCOMITANT RELATIONSHIPS *Accessory meanings*
gination		Excitement	Excitement.
ly imagination	Imagination		Pride, candour.
trained nagination			Moderation.
simulation	Humility	Hypocrisy	Weak imagination.
uism	Benevolence	Kindness	Easy to get on with.
uism confined o one's own amily.			Partisan spirit.
itement, nadness.			Enthusiasm, lack of judgment.
elessness	Simplicity	Disorder	
ler	Judgment	Moderation	Reason.
e based on omparison.	Pride based on comparison	Pride based on comparison	Dignity, distinction.
rity, tidiness.	Clarity	Distrust	Prudence.
trust			
son	Justice, loyalty	Firmness	Positive mind.
ety			Gracefulness.
elessness			Absent-mindedness, flippancy.
iness	Preciseness	Attention to minute detail	
acity			

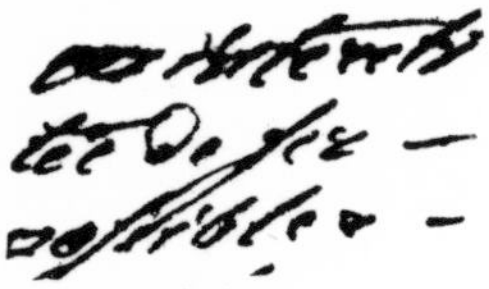

84

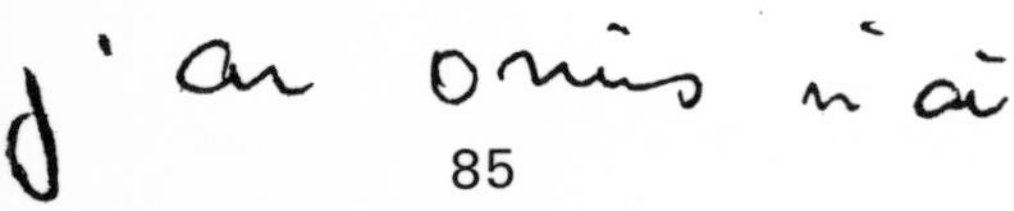

85

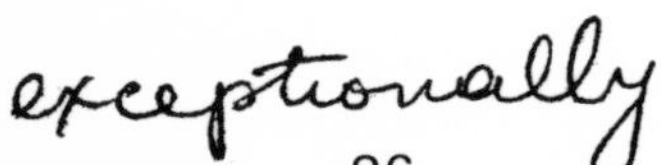

86

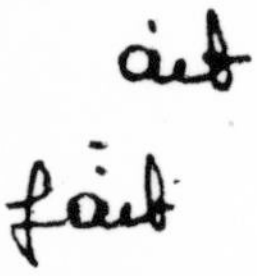

87

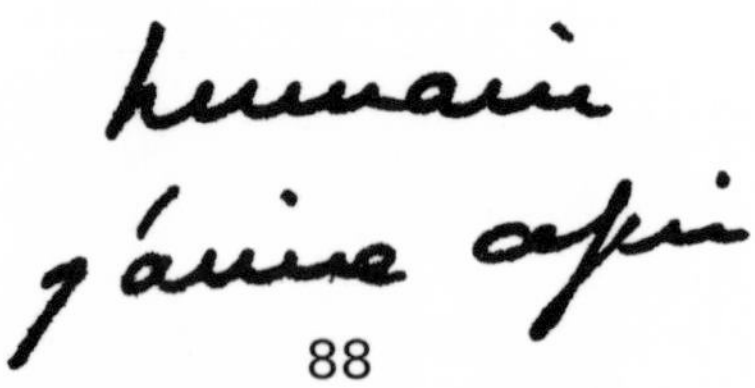

88

89

situated very high up
placed before the
  letter (87) . . . . . .
placed behind the
  letter (88) . . . . . .
very light . . . .
accentuated . . . . . .
after the signature (8
in the wrong place,
  thick. . . . .
in the wrong place,
  light and scattered
in the wrong plaće,
  at the beginning o
  sentences . . . .
Misuse of exclama-
  tion, interrogation
  and suspension
  points . . . .
frequent *Underlining*
Margins missing. . . .
well arranged . . . . . .
right and left . . . .

INARY MEANINGS	MEANINGS *more specifically relating to* *general superiority*	*general inferiority*	CONCOMITANT RELATIONSHIPS *Accessory meanings*
gious spirit			Mysticism.
ntaneity			Spirit of initiative, vivacity.
k of ardor			Timidity.
cacy	Delicacy	Weakness	Firmness.
eriality			
dence	Prudence	Distrust	
sity			
athing troubles			Asthma, oppression.
itation			Pause for thought, a difficult notion.
ggeration	Enthusiasm	Lack of	Imagination, excitement, madness.
ggeration	Enthusiasm	judoment	Imagination, excitement, madness.
k of good taste			Economy.
od taste			A feeling for art.
icate person.			

8. Study of the letters from A to Z.

The closer a letter is to the standard shape, the more harmonious it is and the more fully it renders the perfection of the intelligent and moral being. Of course, this applies to letters which are instinctively formed rather than to those which are written in a calligraphic style.

When the letter is distinctly odd, untidy or crudely formed, it is inharmonious, and conveys an image of spiritual disorders.

Any diagnostic observation of handwriting samples should be based on this principle.

The handwriting of a strong, well-formed character is always in keeping with this rule; it bears the seal, as it were, of normality and harmony.

The handwriting of lower, insensitive, unintelligent types, with disorderly minds, all bear the mark of disharmony.

Accordingly, the closer a hand comes to the harmonious type, the more beautiful it will be, and, conversely, the more it resembles the inharmonious types, the more it will tend to represent imperfections, defects, and departures from independence of spirit, intelligence and sensitivity.

Let us consider two examples.

Jean-Jacques Rousseau was a first-class writer. His handwriting is harmonious and shows a truly superior intelligence (fig. 90).

If we take a random example of the handwriting of a more ordinary mind, an intelligence absorbed by the making of money, that of a businessman, for example, we shall see immediately the clear distinction between a harmonious and an inharmonious hand (fig. 91).

Of course, we could have chosen samples of much cruder handwriting than this, revealing natures far more commonplace than his; however, this sample will suffice to illustrate the distinction we are making.

A study of the letters in detail will enhance the reader's understanding of these distinctions.

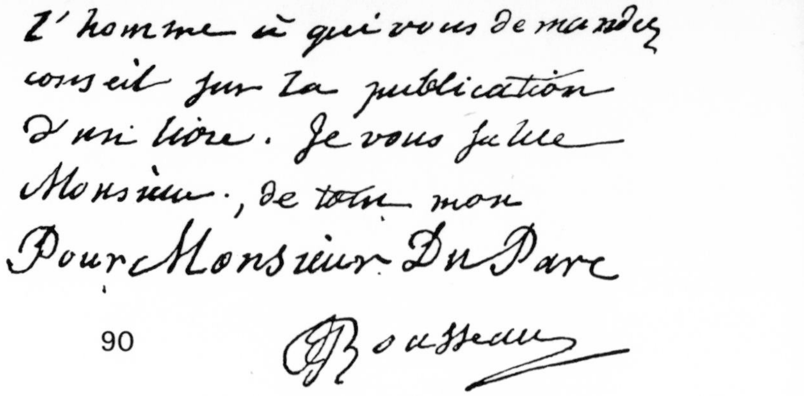

90

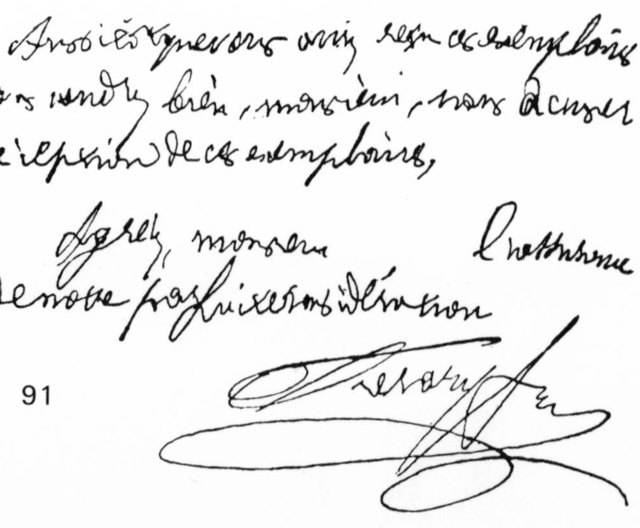

91

In graphology, a letter or a sign has no value in itself. It means something only in its context and when considered as a representative of a particular graphic type.
Even so, each letter has its movement. The typical gesture which formed it gives a symbolic image of the main features of the person's character. Our comments represent that image.

A

Like all other letters, the letter A may come in three positions, initial, intermediate or final.

This is a letter with which few basic signs are associated.

Capital A occurs only rarely in handwriting; in many cases, it is written clumsily. A well written, harmonious A is a sign of intelligence, and a cultivated mind.

1. Very harmonious letter. (Goethe).

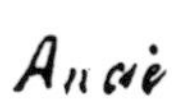

2. Harmonious letter modelled closely on typographic form: poetry.

3. Erect capital letter, inharmonious letter; lack of good taste.

4. Harmonious letter, perfect oval: simplicity, clarity of thought. (The writer Lamennais).

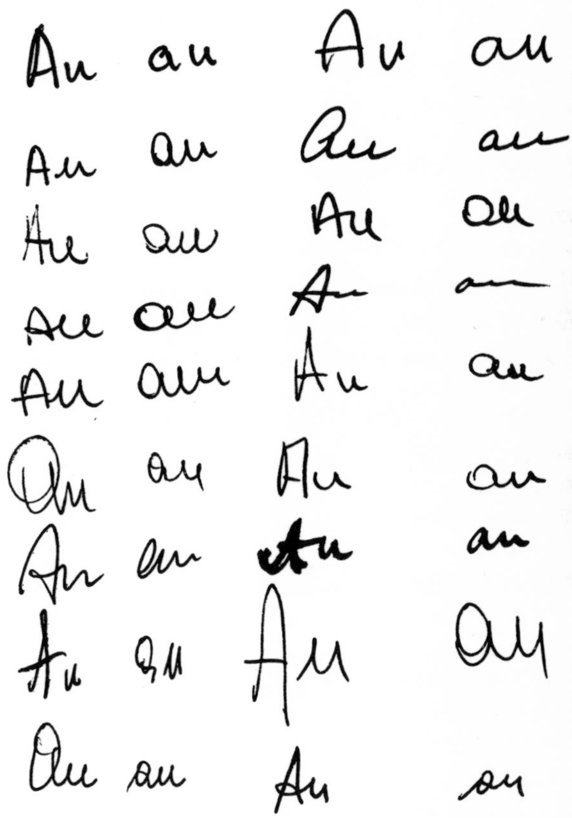

A/ capital. Its resemblance to a roof or a ladder is the basic trait from which the writer proceeds. When arched, it means a person is seeking some special effect, while a narrow, pointed shape is a sign of dryness.
A/small. Open – a somewhat extrovert character. Closed – the opposite tendency. Double loop – doubtful sincerity.

B/capital. The height of the letter and the size of the loops are directly related to the importance the individual attaches to himself. The extent to which it is joined to or separate from the next letter indicates the degree of a person's sociability.
B/small. The variety of shapes, the height and the nature of the join to the next letter have the same meaning as in the case of the capital.

B

Like the capital A, capital B is often clumsily written. When it is regularly formed and not extravagant, modelled on the typographic letter, it is a sign of a cultivated mind, with a taste for beautiful things and a poetic sense.

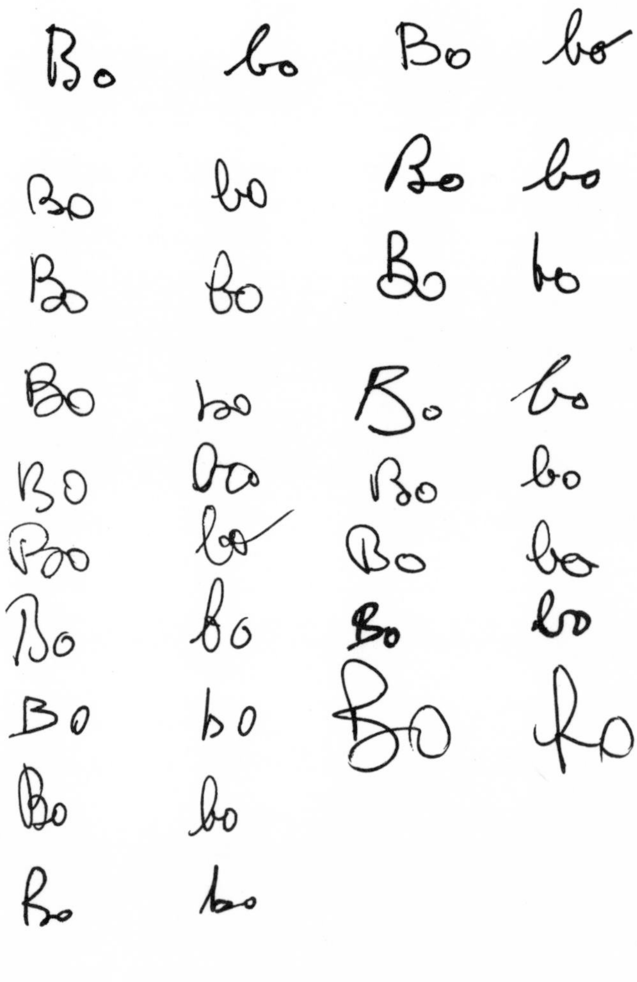

1. Harmonious capital: a dreamer, with Utopian ideas, and a sense of poetry. (Babeuf).

2. Capital letter: a tenacious person; angular handwriting (A bishop).

3. Inharmonious capital: pretentiousness.

4. Harmonious capital: cultivated mind, a serious writer, a scholar or critic.

5. Inharmonious capital, far-fetched: *pretentiousness.*

6. Completely inharmonious capital; sheer vulgarity, no feeling for beauty. (A woman).

7. Inharmonious capital: exaggeratedly tall letter, partly thick and blurred, partly slender; *sufficiency.*

Small *b* carries no basic signs other than those normally associated with the other small letters.

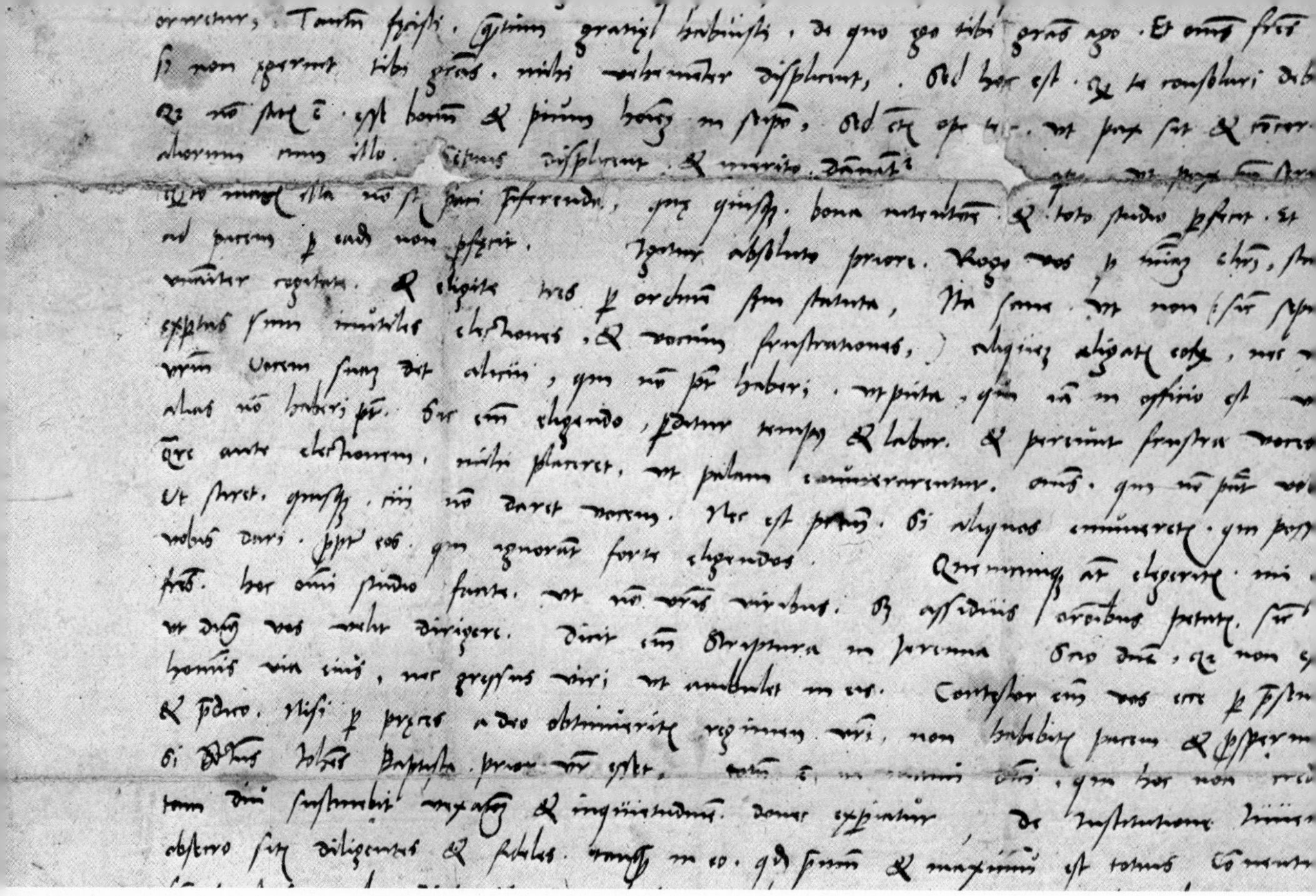

oriretur, Tamen fecisti, cujus gratias habuisti, de quo ego tibi gratias ago. Et quis sic
si non egerunt tibi gratias, mihi vehementer displicent, Sed hoc est, ut te consolari de[bi]
re non stet [illegible] est bonum & pium hoc in te ipso, Sed [illegible], ut [illegible] & [illegible]
aliorum cum illo. [illegible] displicent. & merito [illegible]
[illegible] ista non est hic [illegible], [illegible] bona [illegible] & toto studio [illegible]. et
ad partem [illegible] non [illegible]. Igitur absoluta priore. Rogo vos per [illegible], [illegible]
[illegible]. & eligite vos per ordinem [illegible] statuta, [illegible] non [illegible]
[illegible] electionis, & variis [illegible], [illegible] aliquam [illegible], [illegible]
[illegible] verum [illegible] alium, quam non [illegible] habere, [illegible]. quam [illegible] in officio est [illegible]
[illegible] ante electionem, mihi placeret, ut palam [illegible]. [illegible]
Ut [illegible] non daret [illegible]. [illegible] est [illegible]. Si aliquos [illegible]
[illegible] dari. [illegible] vos. qui ignorant [illegible] eligendos. [illegible] ut eligeretis [illegible]
[illegible] hoc omni studio [illegible], ut non [illegible]. [illegible] assiduis orationibus [illegible]
ut deus vos velit dirigere. Dicit enim Scriptura in [illegible] [illegible], [illegible] non [illegible]
[illegible] viri, nec gressus viri; ut ambulet in eis. Contestor enim vos [illegible]
& [illegible]. nisi per preces a deo obtinueritis regimen viri, non habebitis pacem & [illegible]
[illegible] [illegible] prior [illegible] [illegible], [illegible] in [illegible], qui hoc non [illegible]
tam [illegible] [illegible] & [illegible]. [illegible], de [illegible]
[illegible] diligentes & fideles. [illegible] in eo. [illegible] & maximum est [illegible]

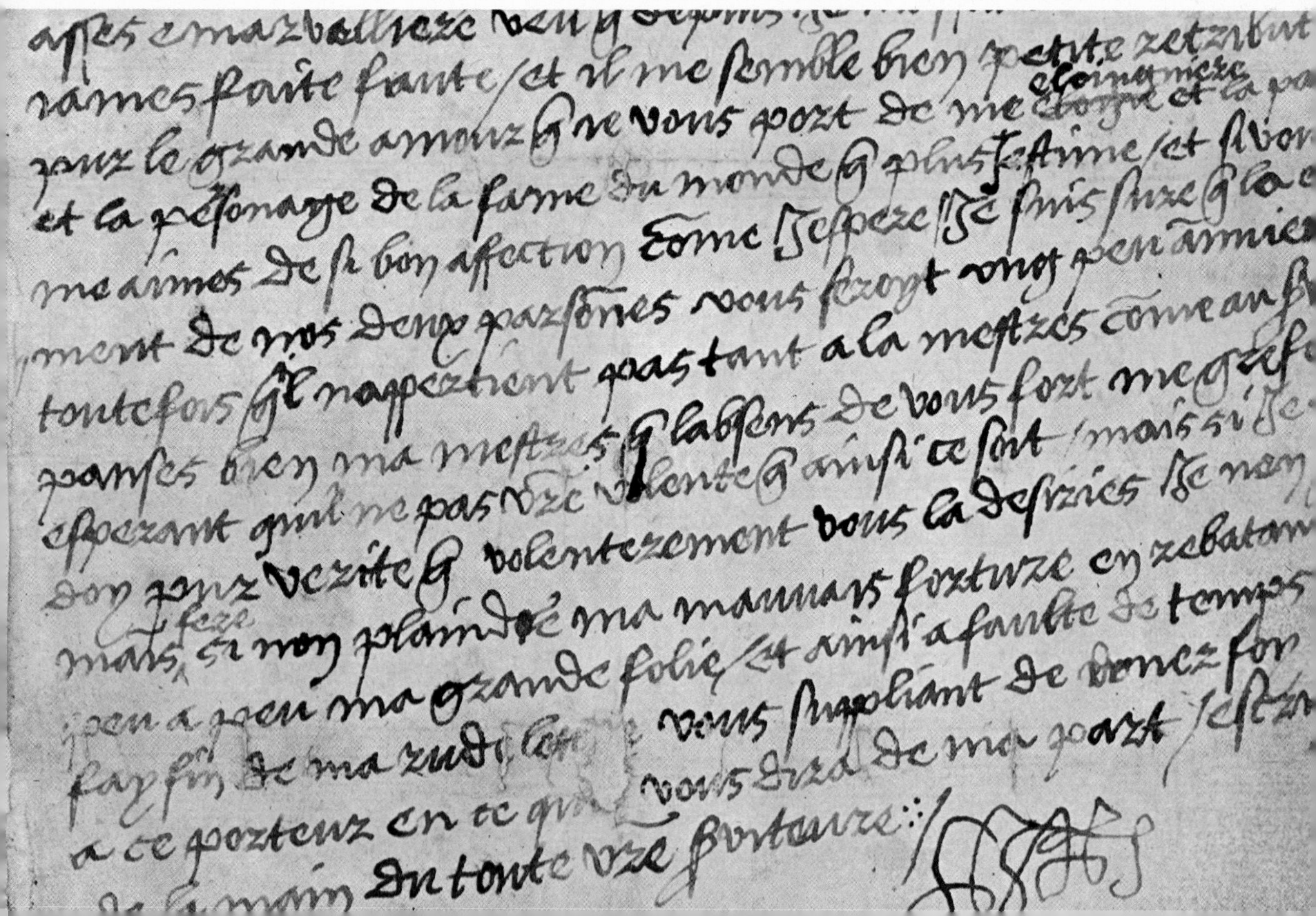

asses en mal heure veu q depuis [illegible]
jamais faite faute / et il me semble bien petite retribut[illegible]
pour la grande amour q je vous port de me eloigner et la pa[illegible]
et la personage de la femme du monde q plus je estime / et si vo[illegible]
me aimes de si bon affection come je espere / je suis sure q la e[illegible]
ment de nos deux parsonnes vous seroyt ung peu ennuie[illegible]
toutefois q'il nappertient pas tant a la mestres come au se[illegible]
panses bien ma mestres q labsens de vous fort me gref[illegible]
esperant quil ne pas votre volente q ainsi ce soit / mais si je
don pour verite q volenterement vous la desiries je nen
mais fere si non plaindre ma mauvais fortune en rebatant
peu a peu ma grande folie / et ainsi a faulte de temps
fays fin de ma rude lettre vous suppliant de donner foy
a ce porteur en ce qui vous dira de ma part / escrit
de la main du toute votre serviteur

A page by the famous Ampère. This is the clear, smooth handwriting of a scientist and a logician. It is also the simple, sober and rounded hand of a shy man, with a sensitive, good heart. His was a vulnerable heart, also, as can be seen from the descending lines.

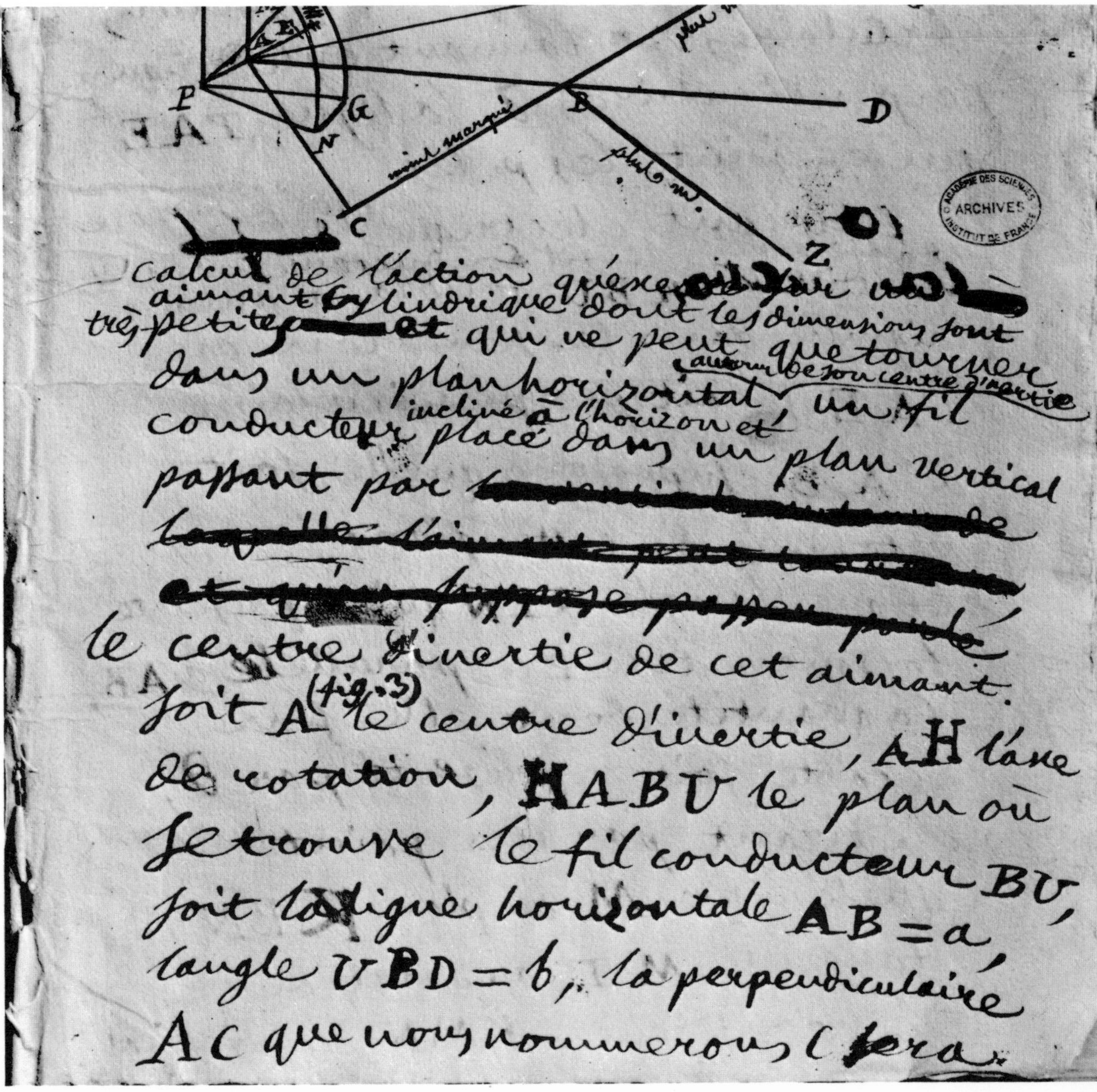

Calcul de l'action qu'exerce sur un aimant cylindrique dont les dimensions sont très petites et qui ne peut que tourner autour de son centre d'inertie dans un plan horizontal un fil conducteur incliné à l'horizon et placé dans un plan vertical passant par le centre d'inertie de cet aimant.

Soit A (fig. 3) le centre d'inertie, AH l'axe de rotation, HABU le plan où se trouve le fil conducteur BU, soit la ligne horizontale AB = a, l'angle UBD = b, la perpendiculaire AC que nous nommerons c sera.

C

Capital C deserves closer scrutiny than most other letters in a sample. It is a treacherous letter. It serves as a trap for the banal, the pretentious and the vain, who, at the first stroke, indulge in sweeping flourishes and scrolls.

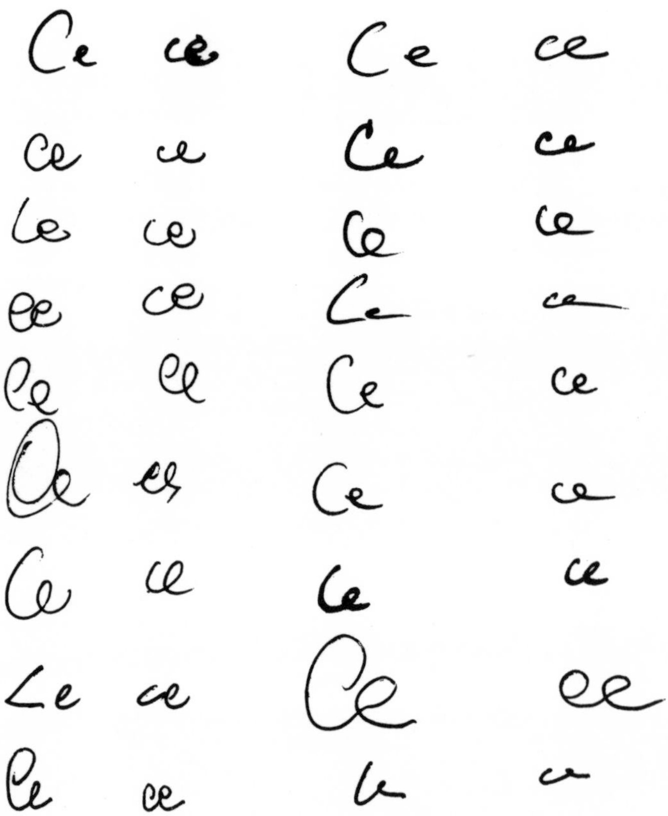

1. Harmonious letter: a sense of beauty, clarity, poetry.

2. Harmonious capital: simplicity; a thick, angular hand.

3. Harmonious capital, spoilt by some scrolls.

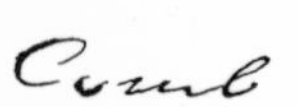

4. Here a capital has foolishly been used instead of a small letter: a banal personality; a soft curve, and, correspondingly, a soft nature.

5. Inharmonious capital C (out of proportion with the letters following it): imagination, ardor.

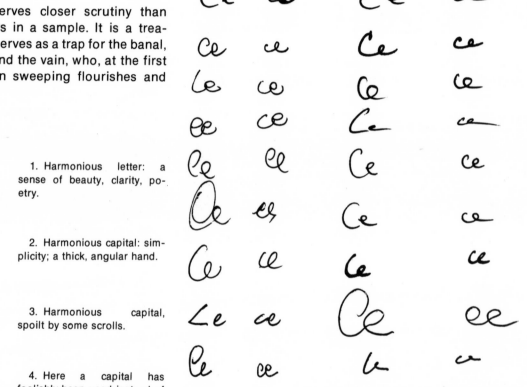

C/capital. Depending on whether it is shaped like a tongs or forms a half-loop, this letter determines to a large extent the outline and the movement of the letters which follow it. The degree of openness, the size and the simple or rolled shape of the C represent modesty, frankness or their opposites.

C/small. This letter lends itself easily to a smooth link with the next letter. If the link is missing, it a sign of inhibition.

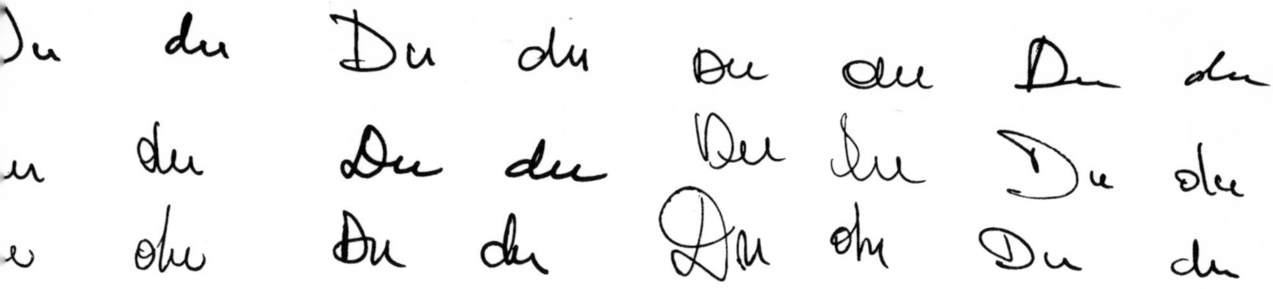

D

Like C, D is a capital letter which is well worthy of particular note in all samples of handwriting. It lends itself to every conceivable movement of the pen, and thus can transmit with equal ease both the tranquil and the irregular impulses of the soul.

In this letter, scrolls can sometimes be seen spreading outwards like flowers at the end of a stem.

Pretentious hooks often occur at the ends of the letter c, whether small or capital.

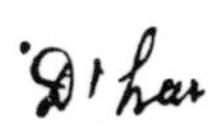

1. Capital D: originality.

2. Harmonious small D: *great* simplicity. Common to all men of great genius.

3. Pretentiousness, stupidity. Crudely inharmonious letter.

4. Small letter, inharmonious. The large scroll, which denotes a pretentious person with an exaggerated sense of his own importance, spoils the handwriting of this modern philosopher, whose reputation is well established.

5. Small D linked to the next letter by a gracious curve descending from the D: *logical sequence of ideas.*

6. Small D ending in a scroll-like hook: vain, pretentious, presumptuous person, with an excess of self-confidence.

7. Intermediate small D, scroll ending in a hook: pretentiousness.

8. Inharmonious small D, with a long reverse curve: imagination.

9. Small D: wild, unfettered imagination.

D/capital. The greater or lesser degree of swelling of this letter indicates the extent of the writer's vanity. Typographic D indicates clarity of thought, while an ornate form denotes a lack of culture and pretentiousness.

D/small. The height of the stem of this letter, its variations from straight to sinuous and its angle of inclination denote the writer's imagination or idealism.

E/capital. A well formed capital E shows how dignified a person is. When shaped like a sigma or a crab, it means rash judgment or touchiness and distrust.
E/small. The small loop of this letter may be more or less constricted; it serves to hold back feelings, sometimes to the point of stifling them completely in an inky knot.

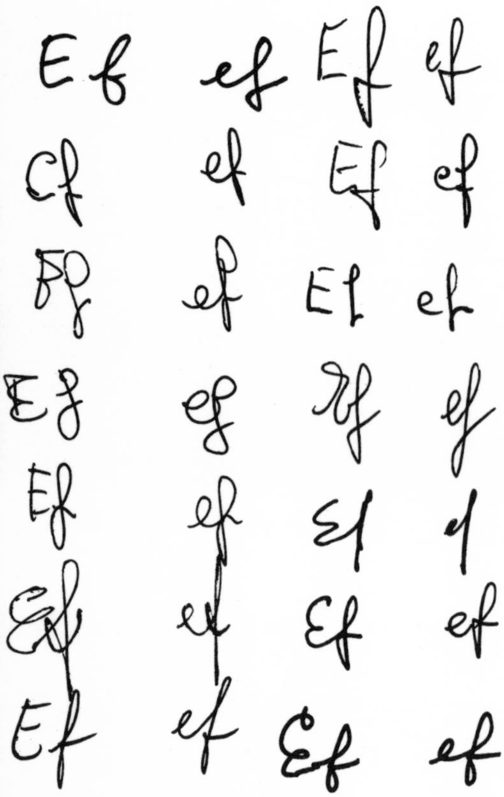

E

Capital E is relatively unimportant: but final *e* figures prominently in our studies, on account of the many forms the pen may adopt for this mute final vowel.

Final e is worthy of the closest scrutiny.

1. Harmonious letter: sense of the beautiful, simplicity, poetry.

2. Harmonious letter in a masterly hand: a feeling of strength.

3. Capital ending in a selfish hook. This hook descends below the inharmonious letter.

4. Small final E: strong will, ardor.

5. Small final E: imagination, excitement.

6. Small final E: impulsive, imaginative person, with little regard for risk. (Cambronne).

F/capital. When formed with a stem and two bars, it expresses strength of affirmative will-power and action. If the upper bar extends beyond the lower, or is situated above the stem, it is a sign of a domineering person.
F/small. The height and shape of the stem, the relative size of the upper and lower loops indicate the degree of intellectual power or of sensuality.

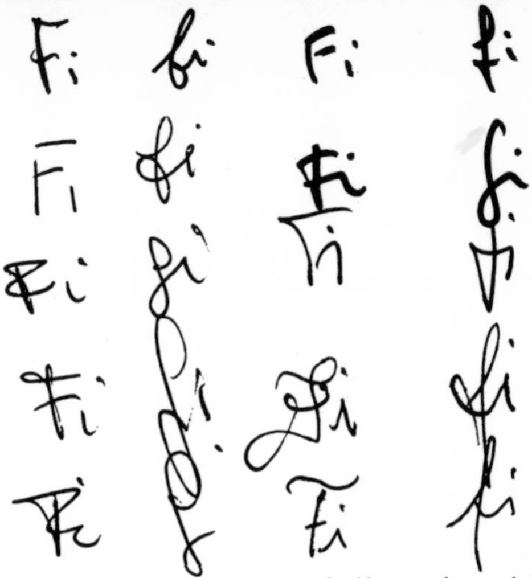

7. Small final E, large reverse link: nonchalance, imagination.

8. Final E replaced together with several other letters, replaced by a line: great sophistication.

F

The letter F also lends itself to flourishes and scrolls, though it occurs less frequently than E.

1. Harmonious letter: vivacity, boldness, gracefulness.

2. Very harmonious letter, barely distinguishable from the typographic shape of the capital F: poetry, conceptual thinking.

3. Harmonious letter very close to the typographic capital F: sense of form. A scholar who has written verse. (Littré).

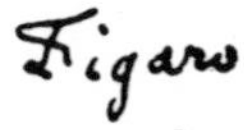

4. Harmonious letter: sense of beauty, boldness. (Berlioz).

5. Capital F similar to the typographic shape: will-power, tenacity.

6. Small initial F, harmonious form: clarity, force, conviction.

7. Small F ending in a single stab-like stroke, in a generally angular hand: affirmation, an energetic person, who has deeply held convictions.

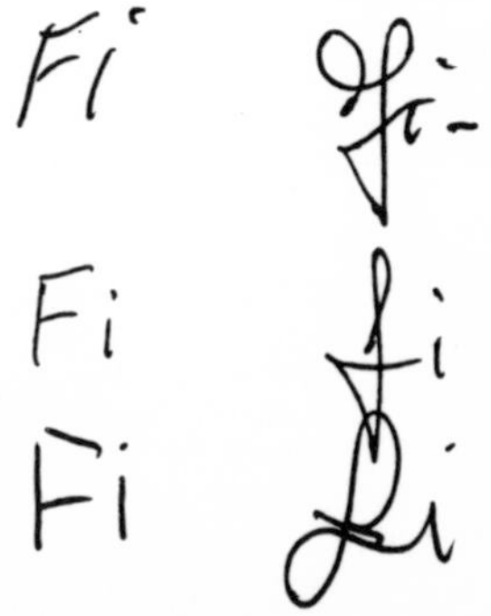

G/capital. The fullness of the body of this letter is a direct introduction to the personality of the writer: vain, if the swelling is large; selfish, if the stroke is knotted; often both at the same time.

G/small. The lower loop of the downstroke can indicate the degree of material appetite and the form of a person's sensuality.

G

G is a letter which is often written with hooks on its upper part, while its lower part is commonly found to have vigorous strokes and imaginative impulses.

When it has enormous loops, it indicates a lack of good taste.

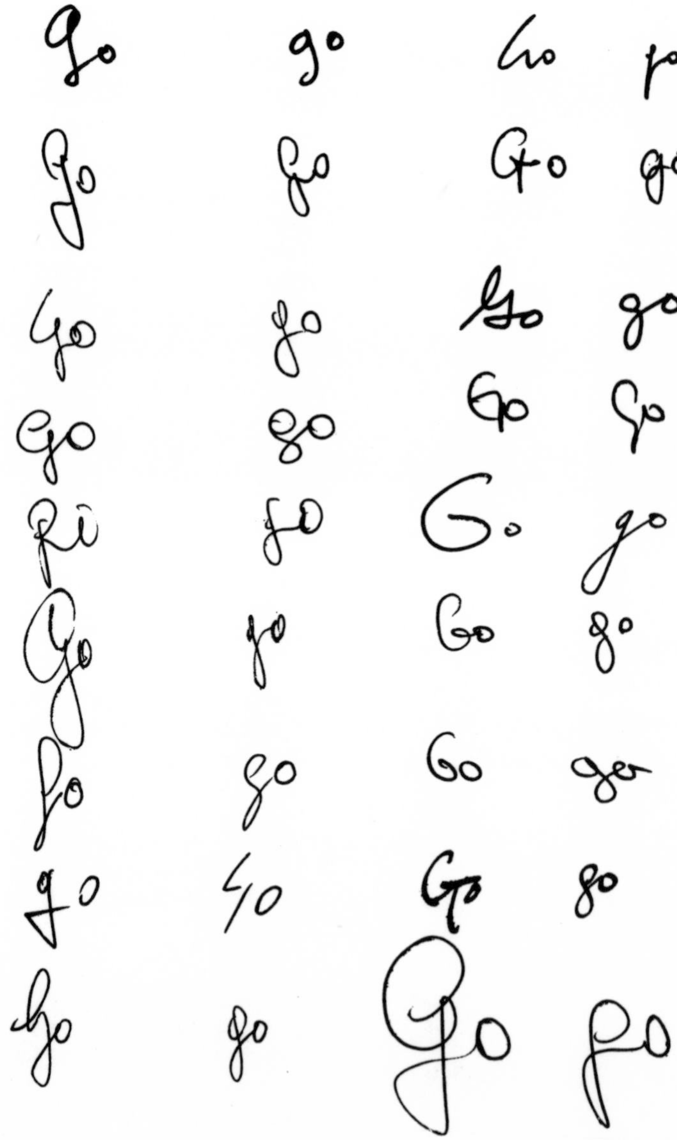

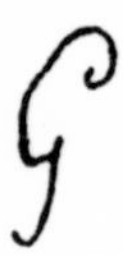

1. Masterly, harmonious letter: lofty sentiments, forceful character (Rossini).

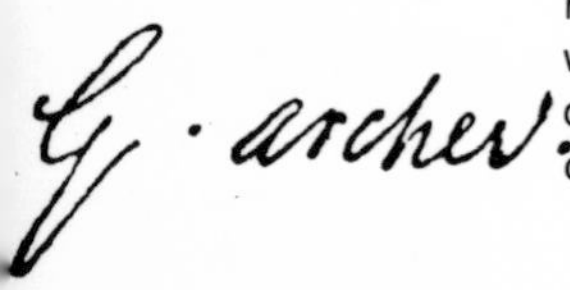

2. Masterly, harmonious capital G: great firmness of character (An Archbishop of Paris, who died on the barricades during a revolution, preaching charity).

H

Harmonious type-like instances of this letter often indicate a poetic sense.

1. Harmonious capital H: lively intelligence, poetry.

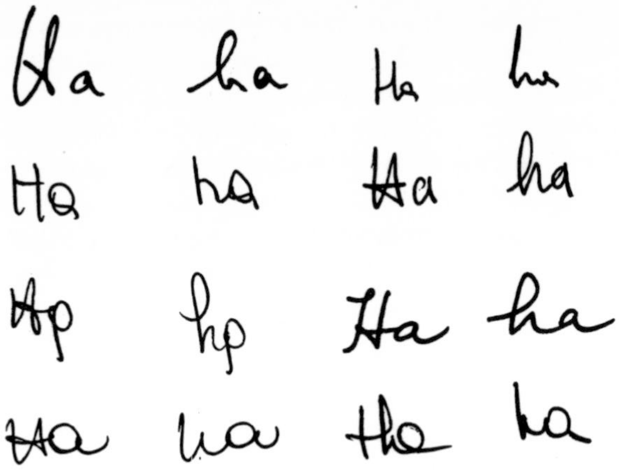

H/capital. Two stakes joined by a bar. A dual affirmation of oneself, strengthened by the will to act.
H/small. The stem may be tall or low, straight or sloping, looped or plain: the relative weight of these features indicates a person's degree of self-assurance.

2. Very harmonious capital H, close to typographic form: poetry.

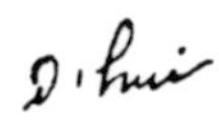

7. Small H in angular handwriting, harmonious, graceful letter.

3. Harmonious capital H, similar to typographic form: poetry. Broken cross-stroke: originality, slightly odd character.

4. Slightly inharmonious capital H: the rounded line of the first downstroke is too sweeping: boldness, originality; the stroke connecting the two downstrokes is a rather peculiar, but graceful curve, and the letter as a whole is quite masterly: impression of strength.

5. Inharmonious, yet lively and elegant capital H: impression of strength, grandeur, gaiety, liveliness (Henry IV, King of France).

6. Inharmonious capital H, downstrokes too close together, too narrow and too tall: prudence, timidity, false situation; a man who has suffered; here we have a soul that is permanently in a state of anguish.

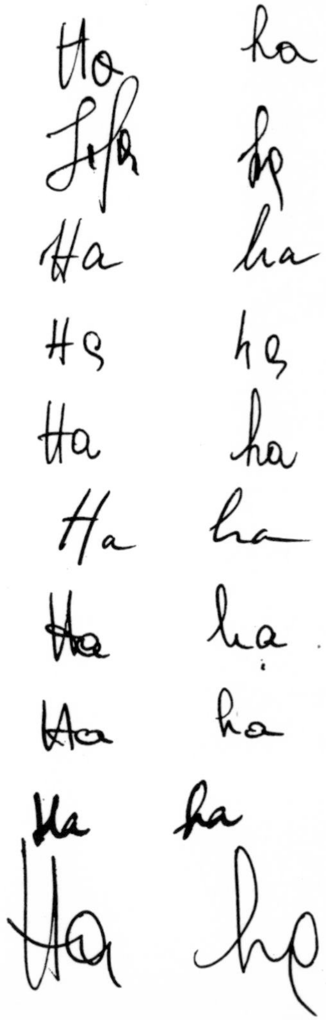

I/capital. The standard schoolroom I, with curves and loops, denotes tradition, convention and sociability, if linked to the following letter. The typographic form stands for free affirmation of one's taste and ideas.

I/small. The dot is the only feature of this letter which imparts some life to it. Without the dot, it is nothing and says nothing.

J/capital. Speaks the same language as the I. The lower loop of the downstroke adds the significance we have referred to under the letter G.

J/small. Like the i, it requires a dot in order to say anything at all. Its downstroke gives it material consistancy; softness or firmness of the person's ego.

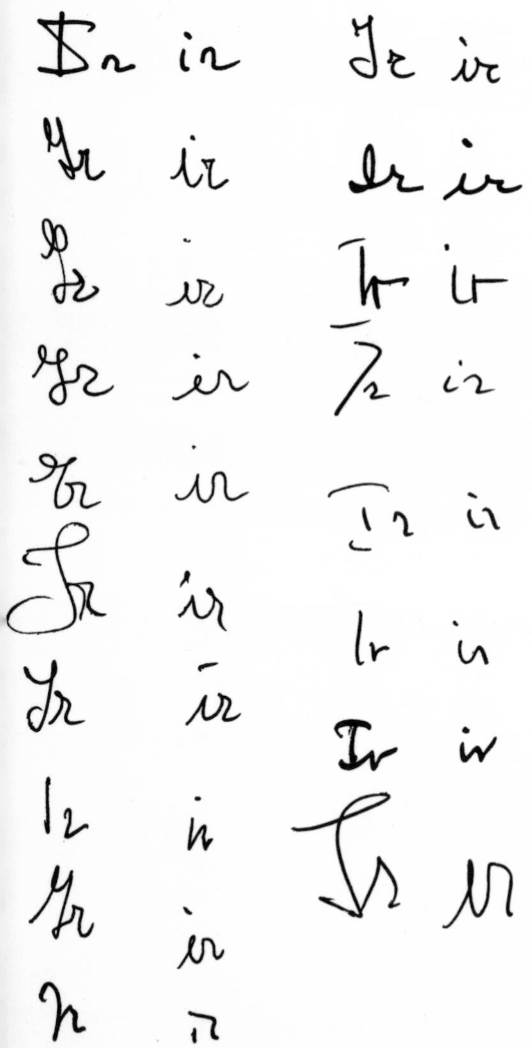

I

From a purely graphic point of view, capital I is relatively unimporant in graphology.

Final small I—quite rare in English—may take the variety of forms associated with final letters, which we shall study in a separate chapter.

1. Capital I similar to typographic form: a person more given to poetry than to philosophy.

2. Harmonious capital I: gracefulness, a feeling for beauty, poetry, simplicity.

J

Depending on the lack of proportion observed in its head and in the final and external outer loops, it may be more or less inharmonious.

1. In this inharmonious capital J, the head of the letter is more prominent than the downstroke: imagination, eccentricity.

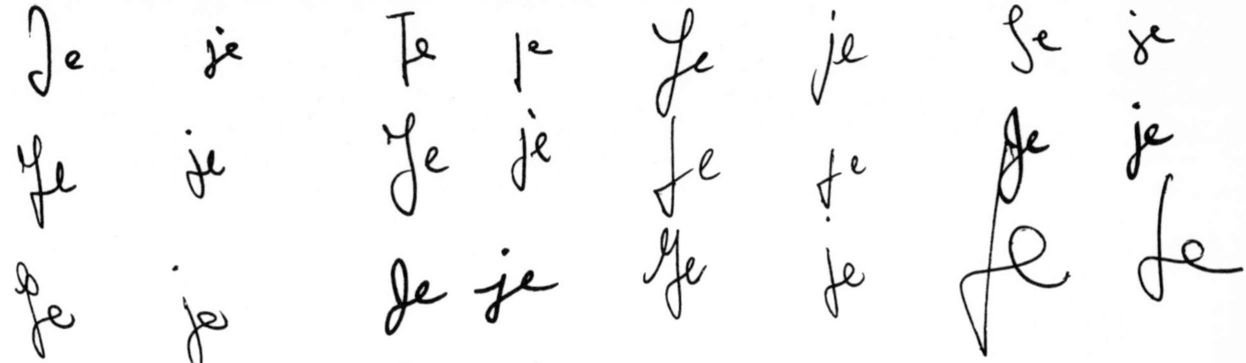

2. Upright capital J: boldness, impression of strength.

3. Inordinately large capital J: eccentric nature, extremely vivacious person.

4. Graceful capital J, somewhat far-fetched, yet petulant: impression of strength.

5. Capital J going too low down, inharmonious: nature lacking in harmony.

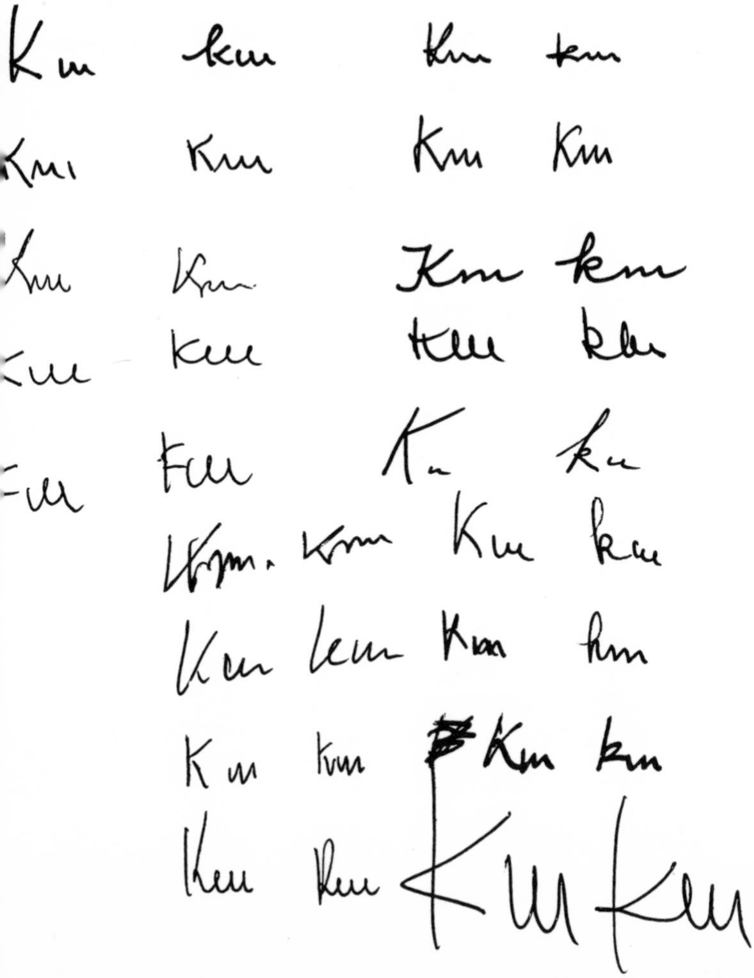

K

The features of J also apply to K.

K/capital. Three strokes: vertical (denoting affirmation), rising and falling. A very living shape, symbolizing the writer's progress through life.
K/small. Same as capital K, except for those who have never really emerged from the schoolroom.

L/capital. The typographic L of the realist is a stem, with a horizontal stroke starting at its foot. Other types of L engage, to varying degrees, in verbal or sentimental flourishes.
L/small. Here the stem is a more or less elongated loop, the significance of which depends very much on the letter to which it is joined.

L

An interesting letter; particular attention should be paid to its upper loop, which lends itself very much to scrolls, and small, selfish hooks.

The small L should not properly be connected, in the front, by untidy loops.

1. Very harmonious letter: a feeling for beauty, simplicity, poetry.

2. Very harmonious letter: gracefulness and intelligence.

3. The lower part of this capital L ends in a hard stroke: energy.

4. Graceful capital L: intelligent, cultivated mind.

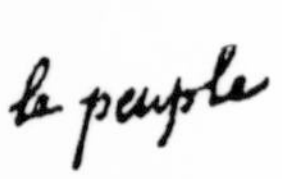

5. Very harmonious small L.

6. Distinguished manners; the rounded shape of the letter is graceful, though slightly pretentious (the letter is inharmonious, in that the lower part of the L should be horizontal, not perpendicular): some originality.

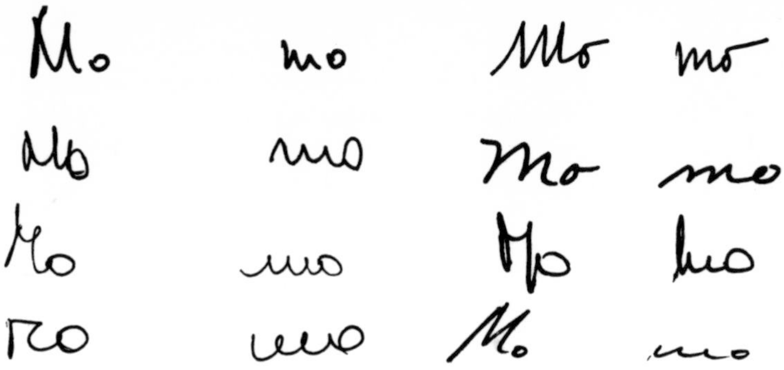

M

Capital M is a crucial letter in graphology, as it is the one letter on which the pen, acting as an unconscious expression of the soul, really enjoys to work. M lends itself to endless combinations of curves, straight lines, connections which may be soft, angular, concentric, florid, with huge loops or descending hooks. A whole book could be filled with the strange shapes which capital M assumes in handwriting.

1. Inharmonious letter, uneven downstrokes: a genius who has fallen short of his ideal.

2. Harmonious letter: a highly developed philosophic sense, simplicity; a thinker.

3. Harmonious letter: precision, a feeling for beauty.

4. Harmonious letter: a feeling for beauty.

5. Somewhat inharmonious letter, uneven downstrokes: stenuous efforts made to achieve an ideal, though often without success.

6. Inharmonious letter; the connection has been made into a curve as big as the letter itself: judgment dominated by imagination; a hook and turn towards the bottom of the line: personality. But for this capital flaw, the first strokes of the letter are harmonious and indicate a cultivated mind.

7. Capital M: Inharmonious capital M, the third downstroke of which is merely a short perpendicular line; the two first downstrokes are graceful: intellectual effort lacking in staying power.

8. Inharmonious letter, backward-facing hook: this is a sign of a certain selfishness; the last downstroke is taller than the others: an impression of strength A perpendicular letter: a prudent man who reveals little of his inner self: an élite mind.

9. This capital M would be harmonious, were it not for the small personality hook: a cultivated, superior intelligence.

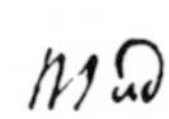

10. This capital M shows, strength, clarity and a sober, restrained style.

11. Inharmonious letter: such a person will be inclined to accord equal weight to superficially glittering things and to those which truly deserve serious consideration; selfish hook; the stroke of the hook is descending; here we have an intelligence which has not risen above the commonplace.

12. Inharmonious letter: the last downstroke of the M exceeds the first, it also has a hook in its upper section which is not found on the first; the lower hook is selfish and the descending line of the hook is a sign of a banal intelligence.

13. This aristocratic M is inharmonious, the last two downstrokes are lower than the first, the initial force of the letter is not sustained; the upper curves are a sign of gentleness; the lower curve of the connection, with its angular shape, suggests movement, will-power, energy.

14. Harmonious letter: a calm, straightforward personality; caution, prudence; the last stroke, forming an angle, shows will-power, perseverance, vigor.

15. Aristocratic M: a person of distinction, high social position, great aspirations, originality.

16. Here we have a nature which often surpasses itself; the last part of the M, which should merely connect with the following letter, is too long; the reverse hook indicates selfishness.

17. This capital M has no connection, and ends in a firm stroke: energy. A very large letter: eccentricity (Cambronne).

18. A prodigal nature. Having completed the second connection of the M, the pen, instead of naturally joining up with the following letter, forms a hook, the symbol of selfishness, and a long reverse curve, in a gesture which seems designed merely to discard ink; a spendthrift, simply showering his money on all and sundry, as if it were inexhaustible.

19. Harmonious letter: simplicity, intuition, penetrating powers of observation and conceptual thought.

M/capital. A measure of pride. If the first downstroke is taller: pride based on one's station in life. Last downstroke taller: pride based on comparison. Joined to the next small letter: sociability.

M/small. Lends itself to garlands signifying flexibility, gentleness. An angular shape denotes coldness, asperity.

20. Imagination which gets carried away; a purely accessory stroke, the connection between the M and the following word is taller than the entire letter, and equal to it in surface area. It is therefore inharmonious. Imagination, eccentricity, and not very reliable powers of judgment.

21. Banal, commonplace; an inharmonious letter. Even though the hook has disappeared in a swift movement of the pen, this negative trait still has the effect of drawing the pen downwards. Despite several outstanding qualities, this is a person who has failed, intellectually, to rise above the common herd.

22. A slightly inharmonious letter: the last downstroke is shorter than the first. This person strives, not always successfully, to reach a certain ideal.

23. Very harmonious letter: strokes of equal height, without scrolls, hooks, coming abruptly to an end; an impression of strength, simplicity, harmonious intelligence.

24. Inharmonious letter, the second downstroke rising less high than the first; struggles towards an ideal; the letter is erect, perpendicular: a clever person. Not wishing to allow others to penetrate his inner self, the writer writes against the natural slope of the hand.

25. A violent and totally inharmonious movement of the pen; the spacing of the downstrokes is grossly irregular: disorder, evil inclinations. The large lower hook is a sign of an undisciplined nature.

26. Incoherent ideas.

27. Here a small letter has been put instead of a capital. This is generally a sign of an incomplete education, sometimes simplicity, a kind nature; it can signify a short attention span.

28. Inharmonious letter ending in a reverse hook the same height as the letter: the accessory has been placed on the same footing as the principal: a lack of harmony in the person's intelligence.

29. Inharmonious letter, downstrokes of uneven height: a person capable of generating bright ideas, but rarely able to carry them through.

30. Very harmonious letter, with fine proportions: clarity of ideas, harmonious intelligence.

31. Very harmonious letter: philosophical intelligence (Diderot).

32. Extremely commonplace, banal personality.

33. Commonplace, ordinary person.

34. Completely, grotesquely inharmonious letter, as the reader can see for himself. A more ungainly shape for a letter could scarcely be found. It is a sign of truly inferior intelligence. At the same time, it belongs to an extremely crafty man.

35. Banality, descending hook: selfishness.

36. Banality, very low order of intelligence.

N/capital. Does the rising arm of the capital cover the small letters which follow it? This is a sign of protection, of willingness to be of use to others, of dedication, though vanity is present to some extent.
N/small. Same meaning as for M. However, garland shapes on this letter make it fairly indistringuishable from u. Gentleness becomes softness, and gives rise to confusion.

N

Capital N also lends itself to a variety of combinations.

1. Harmonious letter: gracefulness, a sense of form.

2. Harmonious letter; small letter in place of a capital: simplicity, sense of beauty.

3. Slightly inharmonious letter, masterly movement of the pen: simplicity, exalted ideas and feelings (Paganini).

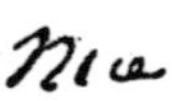

4. Small N used instead of a capital: simplicity, gracefulness. Harmonious letter.

5. This final small N is written with strength of will, indomitable energy.

6. Even tough it is used here instead of a capital, this graceful N means: a witty person.

7. Gigantic capital N, well out of proportion with the other letters: peculiar personality, eccentricity bordering on madness.

O/capital, small. This letter is a loop containing a fleeting, transitory moment – thoughts, emotions or sentiments. Depending on whether it is open or closed, it means frankness or discretion. When closed with a loop, it means discretion bordering on ulterior motives or outright lies.

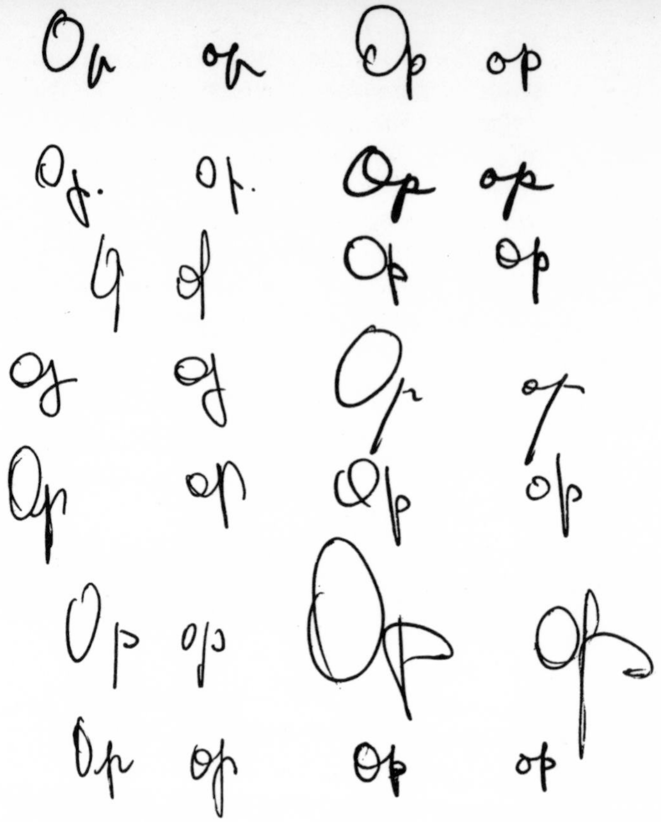

O

Capital O lends itself but little to varied combinations. It follows the laws of inclined or vertical consonants, of normal or exaggerated size.

P

Like capital L, capital P gives rise to a host of unusual forms.

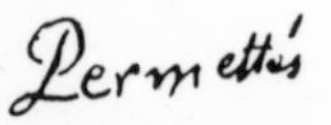

1. Harmonious capital: sobriety, simplicity, order.

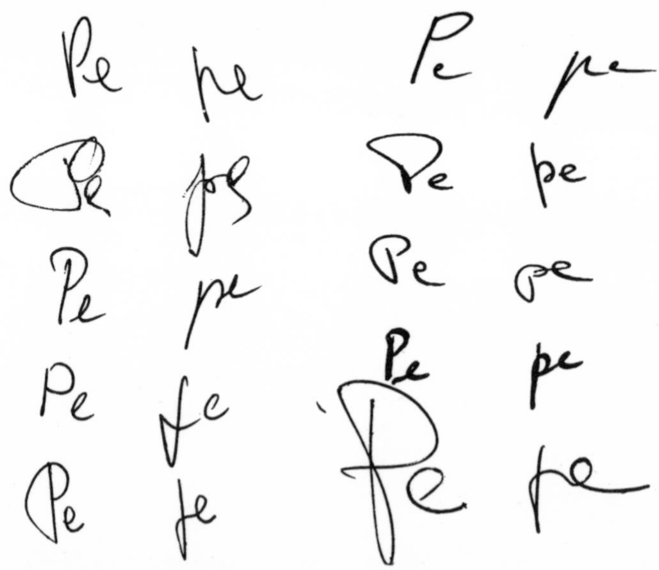

P/capital. The extent of a person's vanity is expressed by the relative size of the head and the elaborateness or simplicity of its shape. This is particularly true if it raised quite high by a tall stem.
P/small. The relative emphasis of the stem of this letter shows how assertive the writer is.

8me Régiment de hussard

strabourg ce 24 novembre an 1808

Cher Mammand je vous ecrie cette lettre pour mainformé de votre santé je vous anvoie ce sertifiquar signé de mai cheffe pour quante je seraie conjé vous presenterai ce sertifiquar. jai aubliyer de vous marquer que dans la route de Vitrie sur marne lon mai doné un billet de logement quil tombé cher un nomai Lafleur le vassard ansien Maitre Boucher ou ses M. Grange il ma dit quil a fait baucoups de comerce a vec vous et il ma tre bien récue il ma dit de vous ferre ses complimens je vous deraie que je suis tres bien au corps et je suis bien a vec mes camarades je vous prie de dire Matante yart dans voige une sentaine de livre de tabac a son fils Garibe Sommer comme un suice

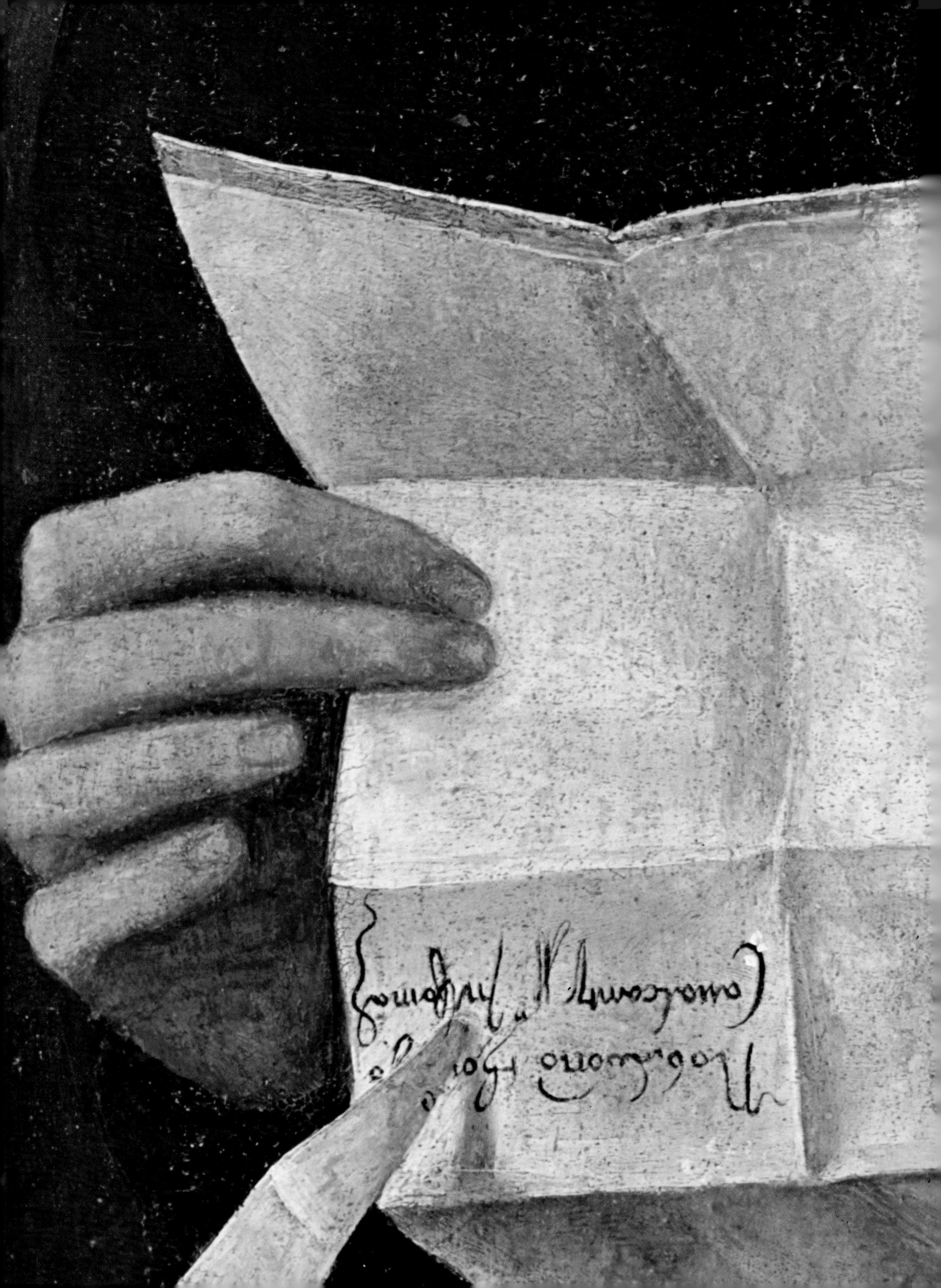

Q/capital. The loop has the same meaning as that of the O. The tail which is attached to it accentuates it or modifies it, depending on whether it is short or deep, shaped like a stem or joins to the following letter.
Q/small. Same meaning as for capital. A low stem on this letter, however, expresses the relative determination of the writer.

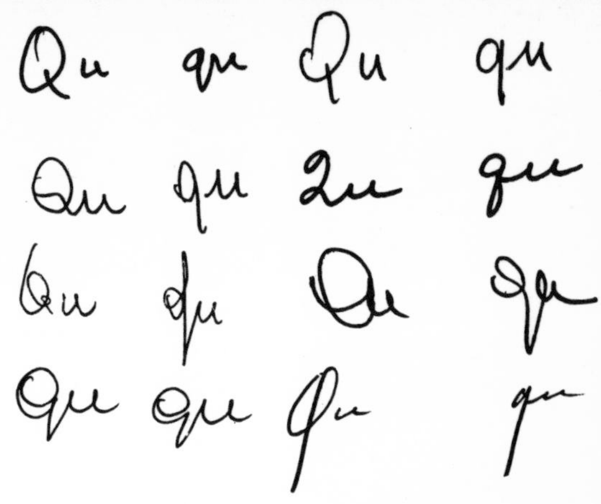

2. Refined intelligence.

3. Inharmonious capital P; an unusual form, with a hard, bold curve; the letter is inordinately big, when compared with the letters which follow it: impression of strength, boldness, attachment to appearances, sense of form, a penchant for contrived witticisms.

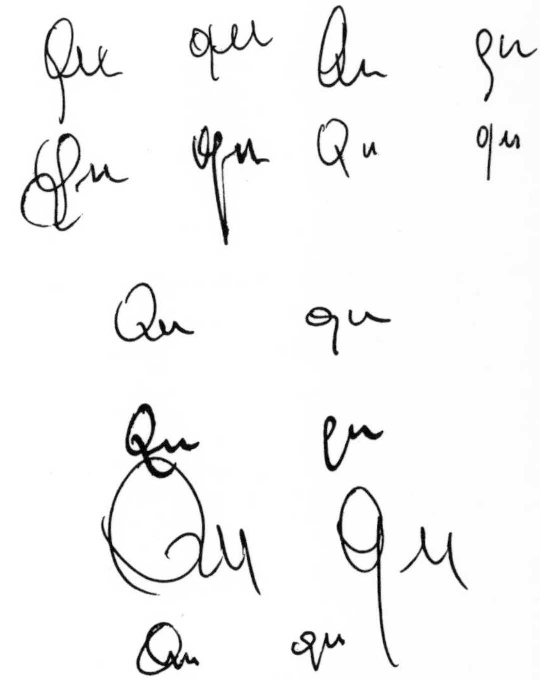

4. Inharmonious capital P (the two lower hooks, followed by the sweep of the pen concluding the upper of part of the letter are clumsy and contrary to the rules of good handwriting), a calculated, pretentious letter: a positivist, lacking in fine aesthetic sense.

5. Inharmonious capital P: extremely vivacious person.

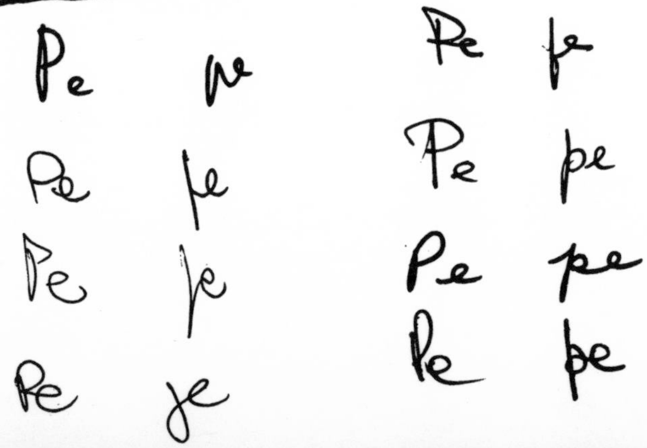

Q

Capital Q occurs somewhat rarely; when used as a small letter, Q follows the rules of vowels, depending on its length and the nature of the connecting stroke.

1. Inharmonious Q, unusual shape: an odd person.

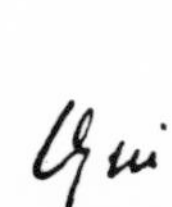

2. Capital Q: originality.

R/capital. The stem and the head are formed with the same motion as that used for the P, and, accordingly, convey varying degress of assertiveness and vanity. The descending arm, whether or not joined to the following small letter, expresses the degree of sociability.

R/small. Quite often the formation of this letter is careless, as it is done in haste. When it becomes so simplified as to be illegible, it is a sign of a casual approach to life.

R

Capital R is well worth studying, as it lends itself to flourishes and scrolls.

1. Harmonious letter: a sense of form, a more poetic than philosophic disposition.

2. Slightly inharmonious letter, the upper part of the head of the R is too big in comparison with the lower part: poetic sense.

3. Inharmonious letter: extreme originality (Rossini).

4. Final small R: a totally inharmonious letter. The head of the letter, in the form of a dot, becomes a swift stroke, not very well rounded, which swings back over the word it is concluding: unbridled imagination, an ardent mind. The abrupt hook which ends the letter is rather stiff: an irritable person.

5. Capital R: imagination, banality, pretentiousness.

6. Harmonious final R: simplicity.

S

Capital S lends itself to every conceivable type of scroll and flourish; it is a letter which enables the pen to indulge in a wide range of eccentricities.

1. Inharmonious capital S; the upper part of the letter is too sweeping; a mind which is impressed more immediately by secondary things than by what is truly important.

2. Final small S ending in a hard line: ardor, perseverance, stubbornness.

3. Small S: vivacity, imagination (Goethe).

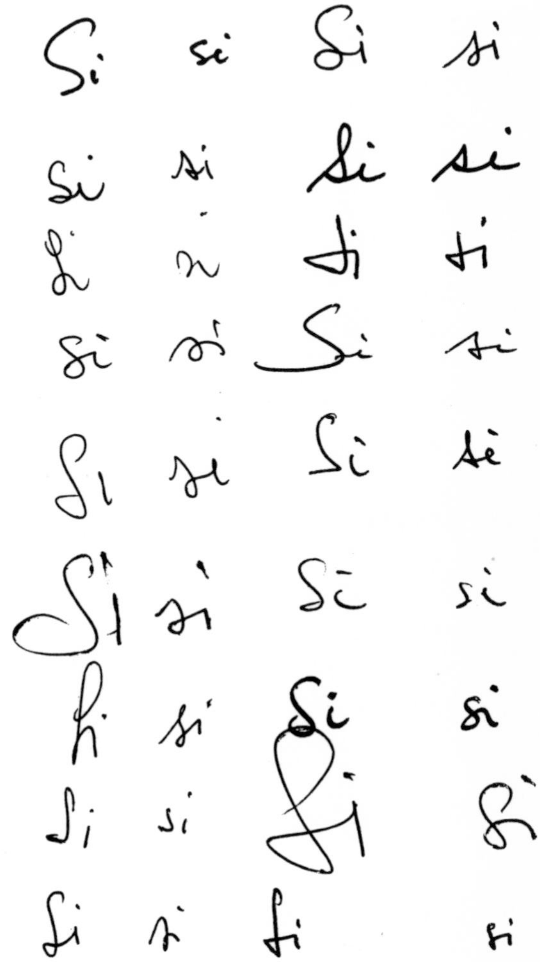

S/capital. Gently curving line means gentleness, kindness, conciliation. The top: imaginative, artistic disposition, independence of mind. The bottom: material inclinations, sensuality.
S/small. It means either memory, logic, fluid thinking, or slowness of mind, hesitation and inhibition, depending on whether or not it is joined to the next letter.

T

Capital T lends itself to a variety of combinations. However, the truly crucial letter in a person's hand is small *t*, because of the countless sorts of cross-strokes which may be found on it.

From the barely perceptible cross-stroke of weak-willed, or mild-mannered persons, to the enormous, thick cross-bars, often ending in a square shape, which are commonly found

T/capital, small. This letter expresses the reflexes of the will. The stem: an affirmation of the ego. Cross-stroke: activity. Height of the stem, position and emphasis of the cross-stroke, constancy or irregularitiy in its shape and position give a clue as to the will-power and the degree of activity of the writer.

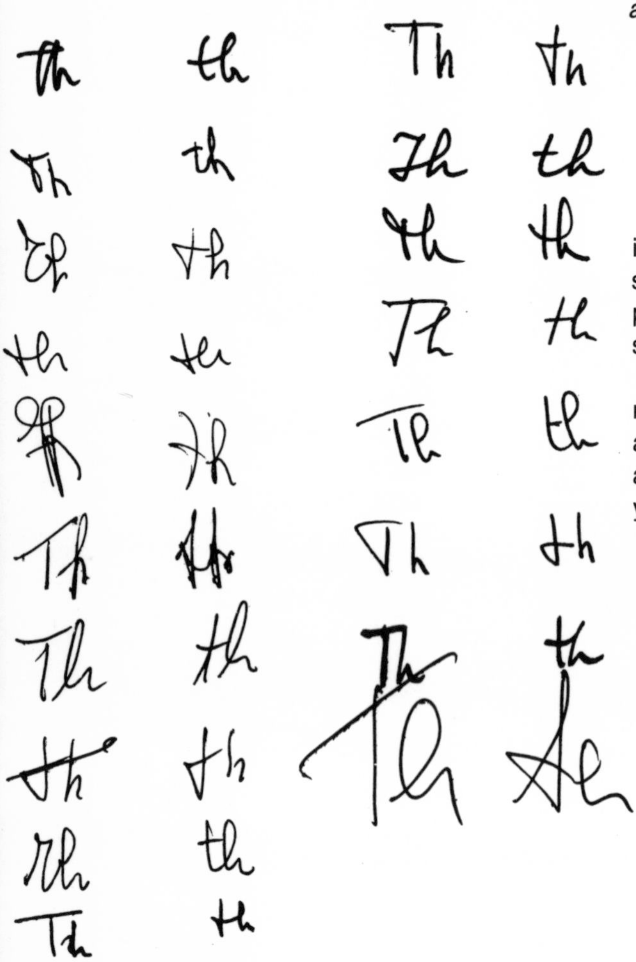

in the handwriting of very strong-willed persons, small t can express virtually all the impulses of the voluntary expression of the soul.

It has been said: ''Give me three lines of a man's handwriting and I will have him hung''; and, similarly, one could also say: ''Show me a letter t, crossed by a man's pen, and I will tell you all about his inner self''.

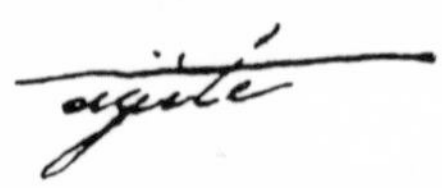

1. Heavily crossed small T: extreme energy and perseverance.

2. Heavily crossed small T: very strong will-power.

3. Heavy and long cross-stroke: impetuous person, with great will-power; very vivacious.

4. Firm, heavy cross-stroke: tenacious person, with the will to persevere.

5. Cross-stroke very high on T: domineering person.

6. Cross-stroke very high on T: great strength of will; a domineering person.

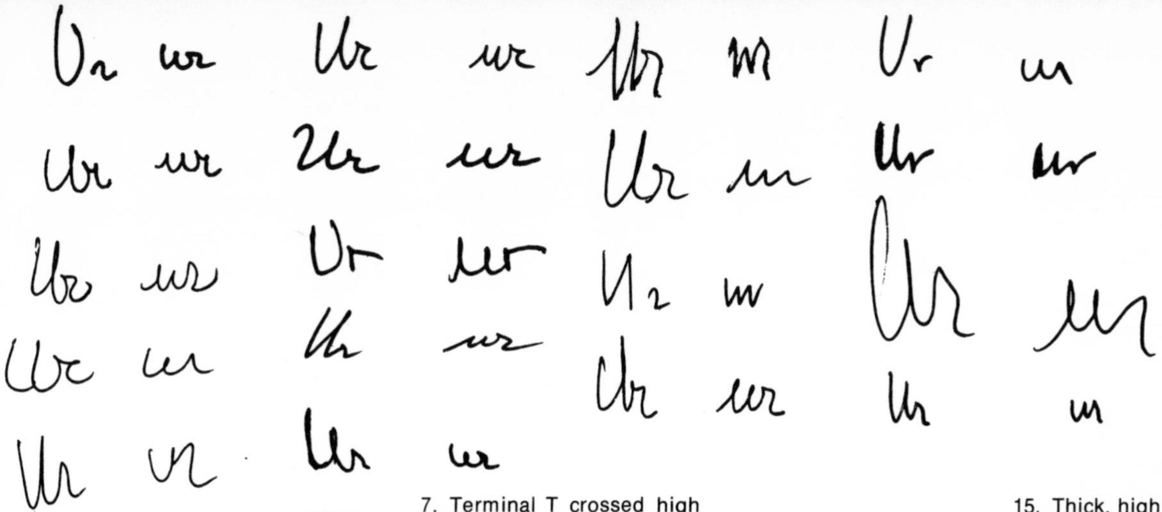

7. Terminal T crossed high up: will-power, a domineering person.

8. Intermediate T ending in a thick, heavy stroke: a stubborn, tenacious person.

9. Small T crossed high up: will-power, a domineering person.

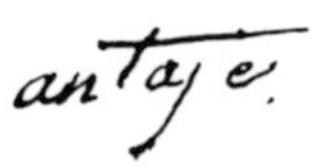

10. A small T crossed high up: will-power, a domineering person.

11. The cross-stroke on this small T touches the top of the downstroke—a classical indicator of the domineering type of person—and the stroke is thick and heavy throughout: extremely domineering person.

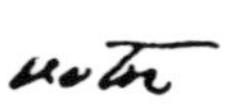

12. Cross-stroke is high, long, thick and heavy: strong-willed person, stubborn, persistent and domineering.

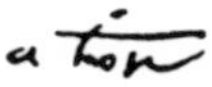

13. Small T: awe-inspiring will-power (Napoleon).

14. Thick, rising cross-stroke, ending in heavy line: energy, perseverance.

15. Thick, high cross-stroke on capital T: domineering person.

16. Long cross-stroke on small T, ending in a hook: stubbornness.

17. Final T: great firmness.

18. Small T crossed with fine, tapering line: a person who frequently shows signs of weakness, and a lack of energy.

U

As a small letter, U follows the law of vowels, particularly in the final position.

U/capital. Open branches, rounded base, with a join to the following small letter means an open mind, frankness, an amiable person. V-shaped branched, pointed base: blunt frankness.

U/small. Same meaning as for the capital. When V-shaped, it may be confused with the m, n and u of angular handwriting; a character lacking in flexibility.

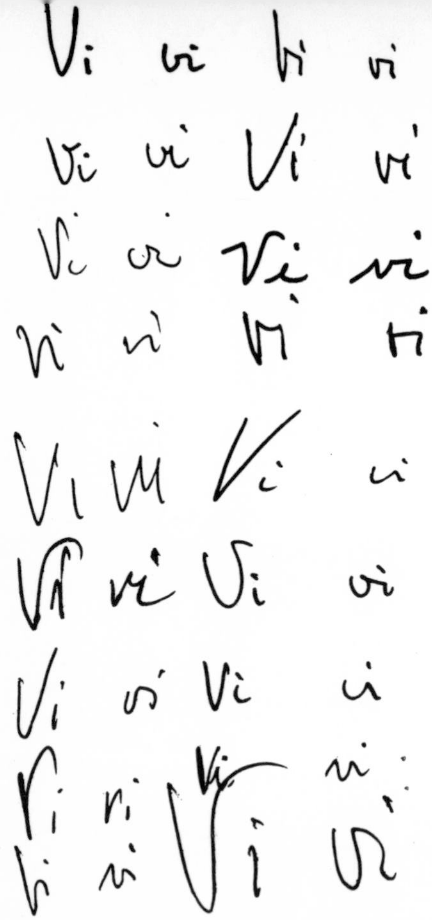

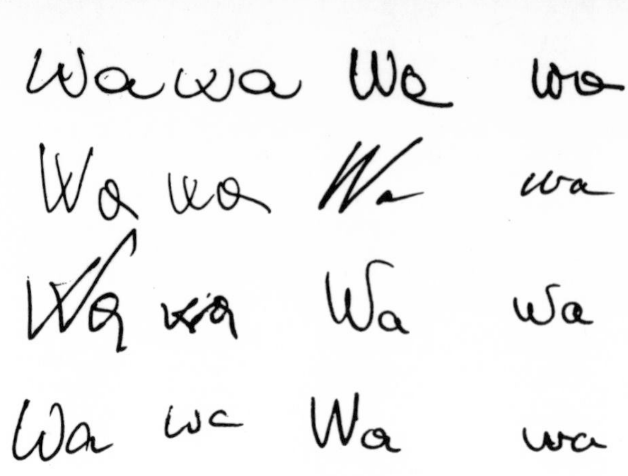

V/W

These letters do lend themselves to certain flourishes, scrolls and odd motions. Consider, for example, the V below.

1. Capital V; a slender, ethereal shape.

2. Capital W: vivacity (Goethe).

V/capital. Speaks particularly through the motion of the rising arm. When this arm is straight, it means rebellion, aggressiveness. When it ends in a curve above the following letters, it means a protective gesture.
V/small. A rounded base can be confused with the letter u; a sign of softness.
W/capital. Like the V, it conveys the person's relations with others. When rounded or angular, it doubles the significance of the letter as a sign of protection or aggressiveness.
W/small. Sometimes assimilated to rounded m, n, u and v, but it is usually possible to tell them apart.

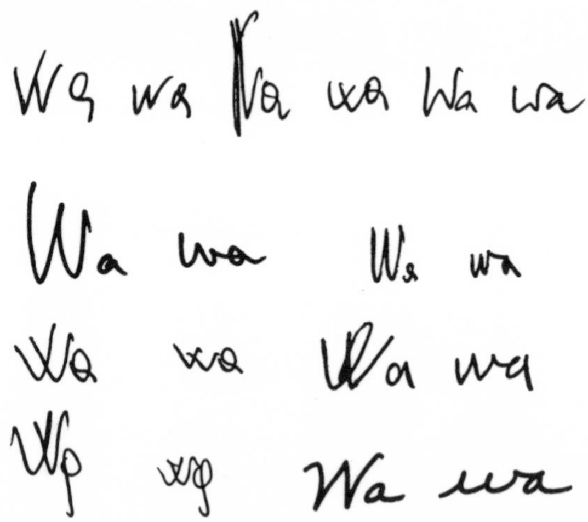

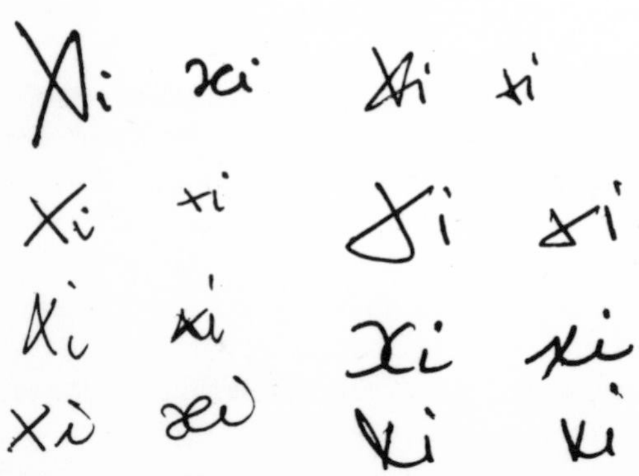

X

Capital X is somewhat rare. Small X follows the law of consonants.

Excessive final X; too high: odd character.

X/capital, small. Its two cross-strokes are the crossed swords of the fighting spirit. The extent to which this spirit is developed in a person can be discerned from the vehemence or moderation of the stroke, and from whether the cross-strokes are straight and bold.
Y/capital, small. This is a V with a downstroke; both letters speak the same language. But the overall significance is emphasized by the nature of the downstroke.

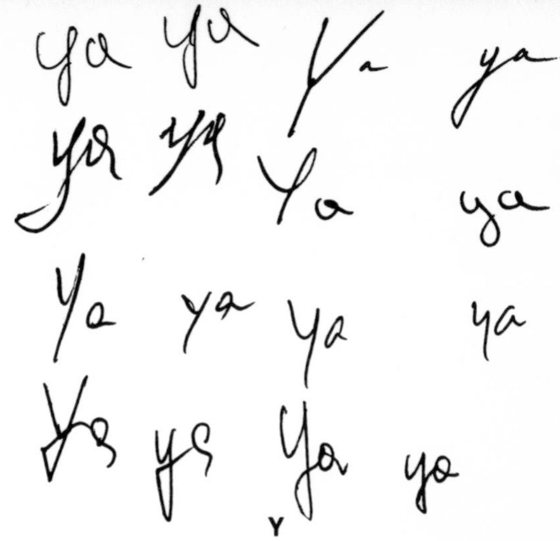

Y

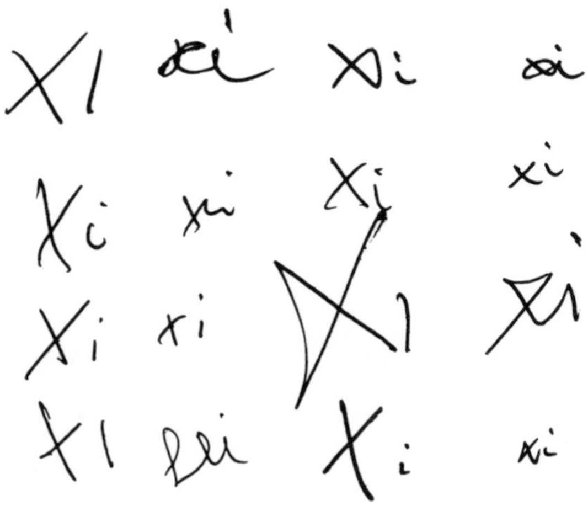

In the final position, its significance depends on the degree to which its lower part departs from the norm.

This capital Y is rather far-fetched, but, nonetheless, graceful.

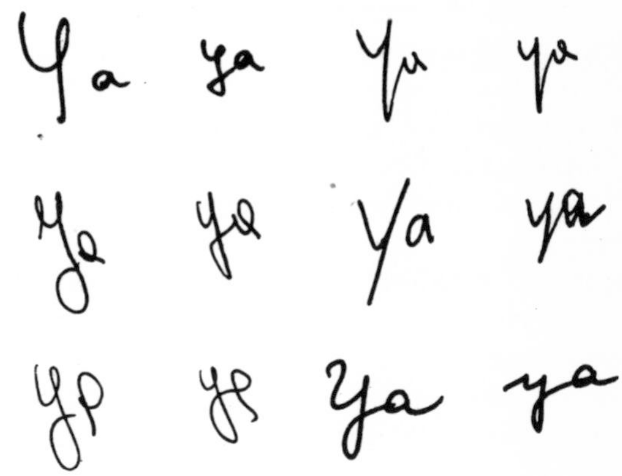

Z

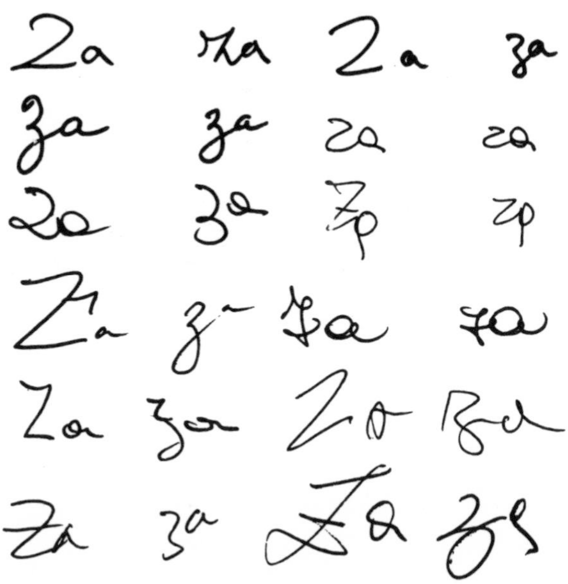

Capital Z is often accompanied by flourishes, though it occurs rarely. Like all final vowels, final Z lends itself to a great variety of movements of the pen.

Z/capital. A commanding gesture. Like a stroke of lightning, it sweeps down in a nervous zig-zag. Only the weak or the sentimental soften it by means of curves.
Z/small. With its downstroke, it assumes a more rounded shape.

1. Final Z: firmness of purpose, imagination. It comes down too far (Voltaire).

2. Intermediate Z; too long: imagination.

9. Final letters.

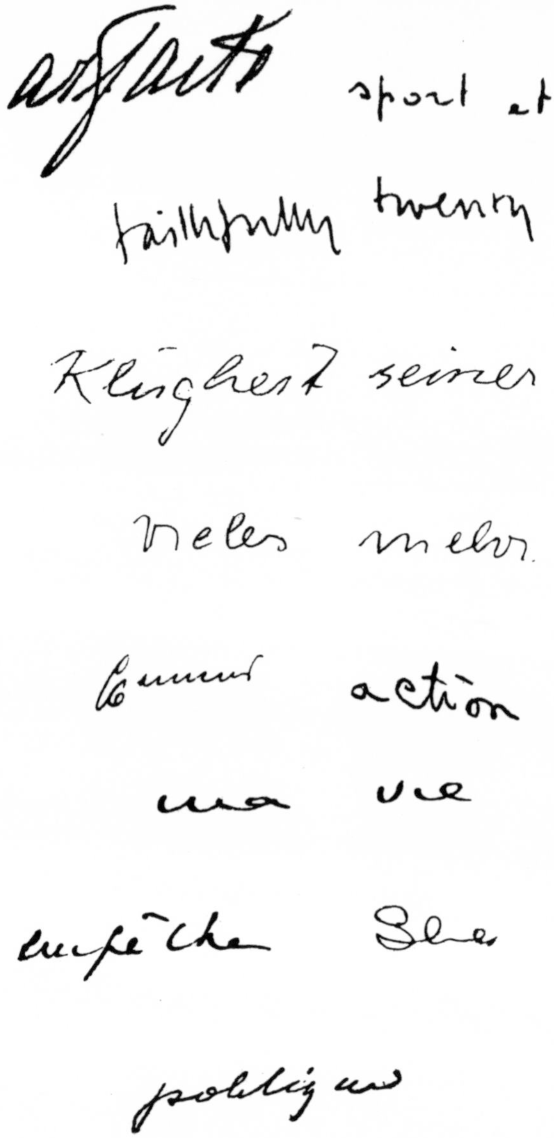

Anyone who has observed samples of handwriting, even without making a very careful study of the subject, will be struck by one quite remarkable phenomenon, which runs directly counter to the rules taught in the classroom by teachers of handwriting: it is that, instead of ending each word with a short line of diminishing thickness, in accordance with the classical model, people tend to end with a sudden, spontaneous movement, which can be quite as diverse as the innumerable types of the human character itself. An apparently insignificant final stroke thus acquires a depth of meaning for the graphologist, who will devote particular attention to final letters in his analysis of a hand.

When final letters end abruptly, and give the impression that the writer was almost afraid to expend his energy, the conclusion to be drawn is that he has a strong possessive instinct, with a marked penchant for economy and restraint—an instinct which may sometimes lead to excesses, such as cheating in the form of corner-cutting.

On the other hand, when final letters are long, rising and rounded, it is usually a sign of great generosity, even prodigality—the kind of person of whom one might say: "The money slips through his fingers." People who are lavishly generous all have this sign; their final letters are long, their words are well spaced out and stretched out along the line. The handwriting of such people is just like a very wide meshed net, through which the coins readily pass!

If final letters are rising, and come at the end of rising words, it is a basic sign of vivacity, which may sometimes take the form of anger and an uncontrollable temper. Anger is a sort of boiling point of the soul, and the rising line

Below: a very curious rough draft of a speech by a politician (Clémenceau).

of the pen seems to translate into visual terms the impulse which has caused the loss of emotional self-control.

All well-rounded, gentle final letters, which have no trace of the acute or the right angle in them, and in which the curve is perfectly smooth, indicate a kind, gentle personality, though one which may, on occasion, also be soft and lazy.

All angular final letters, forming a more or less acute angle with the body of the letter, suggest a lively, headstrong personality. In fact,this is the universal type of the tenacious mind—the kind of mind, which, having once admitted an idea, does not readily let it go.

Soft, rounded final letters also indicate a refined, elegant personality, with a sense of form.

Final letters in which the curves consist of broken segments, as if the pen has tried to form several angles at the same time, are a sign of poor taste, of a Philistine. There is an element of coarseness, selfishness and malice about persons using such angles.

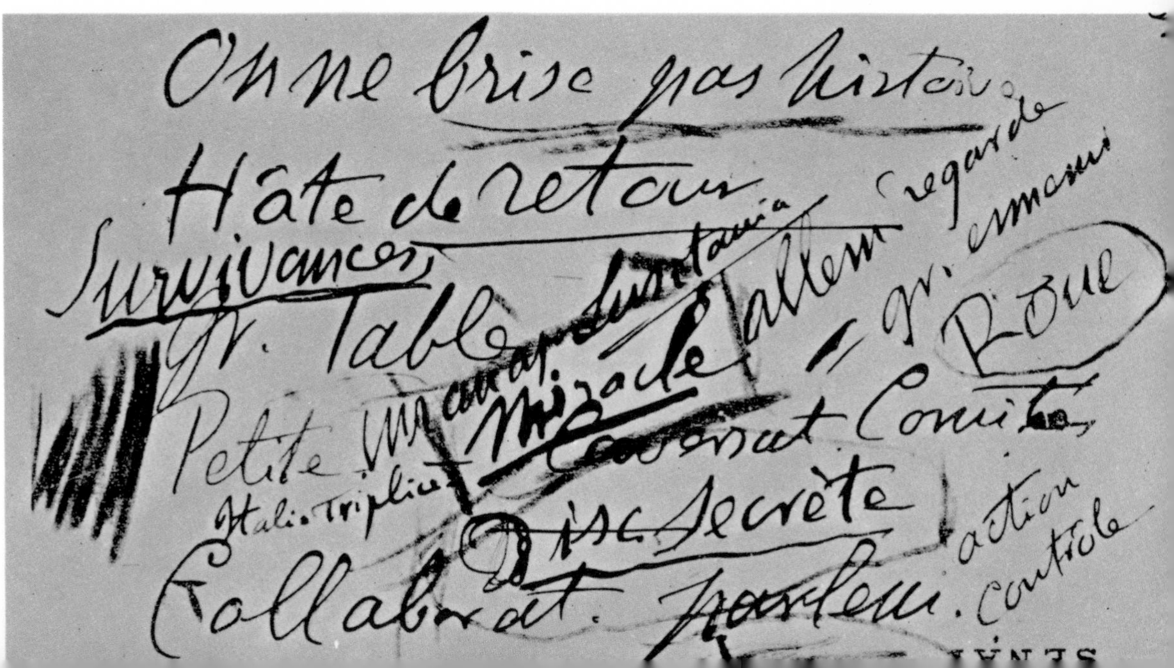

The limpid signature of a great poet.

10. Signatures and related flourishes.

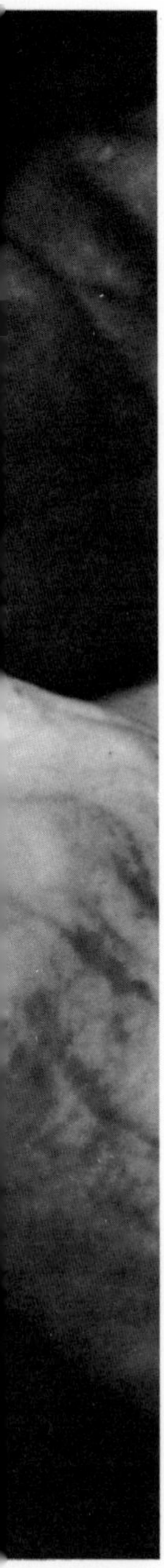

92

93

Let us compare the signatures of two composers: Spontini and Beethoven (fig. 92, 93).

Both were masters of their art; yet, it is easy to see that one lacks the genius of tenderness and feeling, and that the other, headstrong, impulsive and capricious, is tormented by that inner fire, that creative originality which Nature grants only to a chosen few.

The signature and its related flourishes are the most revealing of all the elements of a person's handwriting.

Let us first consider several general characteristics. An unaccompanied signature may reveal that a person is mediocre, or a nonentity; or it may show that he is proud, or sophisticated; in most cases, however, it is evidence of simplicity.

When followed by a period, it is a sign of prudence, and, in extreme cases, of distrust.

This distrust is definitely indicated by a signature after which the writer puts a line followed by a series of dots.

A straight line under the signature means pride.

A curve under the name: self-satisfaction.

A stroke from right to left: a defensive person.

A stroke from left to right: aggressiveness.

If the accompanying flourish goes from right to left, and then back to the right, it is a sign of defensiveness turning to aggressiveness (fig. 94).

A flourish which zigzags across the paper like a streak of lightning is a sign of great activity.

Some signature flourishes look rather like a spider's web: this is a sign of a clever businessman (fig. 95).

If the flourisch completely surrounds the name, it is safe to assume that the writer is, by nature, very reserved, and, in many cases, selfish.

A flourish which, while surrounding the name, leaves an opening, denotes selfishness (fig. 96).

If the name is squeezed between two bars, and linked to one of them (the cross-stroke on the letter T often serves as a pretext for such a connection) it is a sign of considered selfishness, and, in extreme cases, of a special aptitude for dissimulation.

A signature flourish which consists of diminishing circles means sophistication and, often, a good head for business.

A curved stroke placed under the name, principally horizontal, means assurance, optimism, happy disposition (fig. 97).

If formed of inter-woven strokes, the flourish denotes a fondness for intrigue.

Any complicated flourish means distrust.

94

95

96

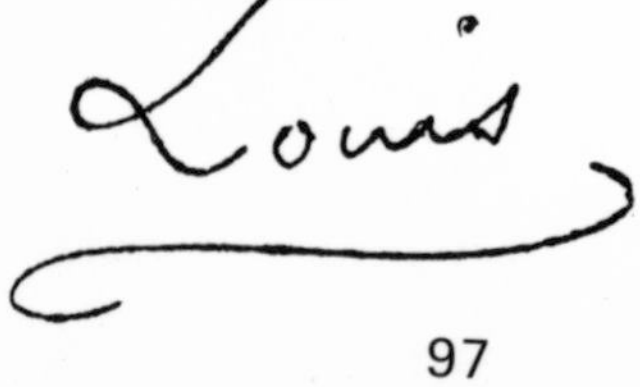

97

The studied impersonality of a business letter often makes the style of the signature stand out in sharp contrast.

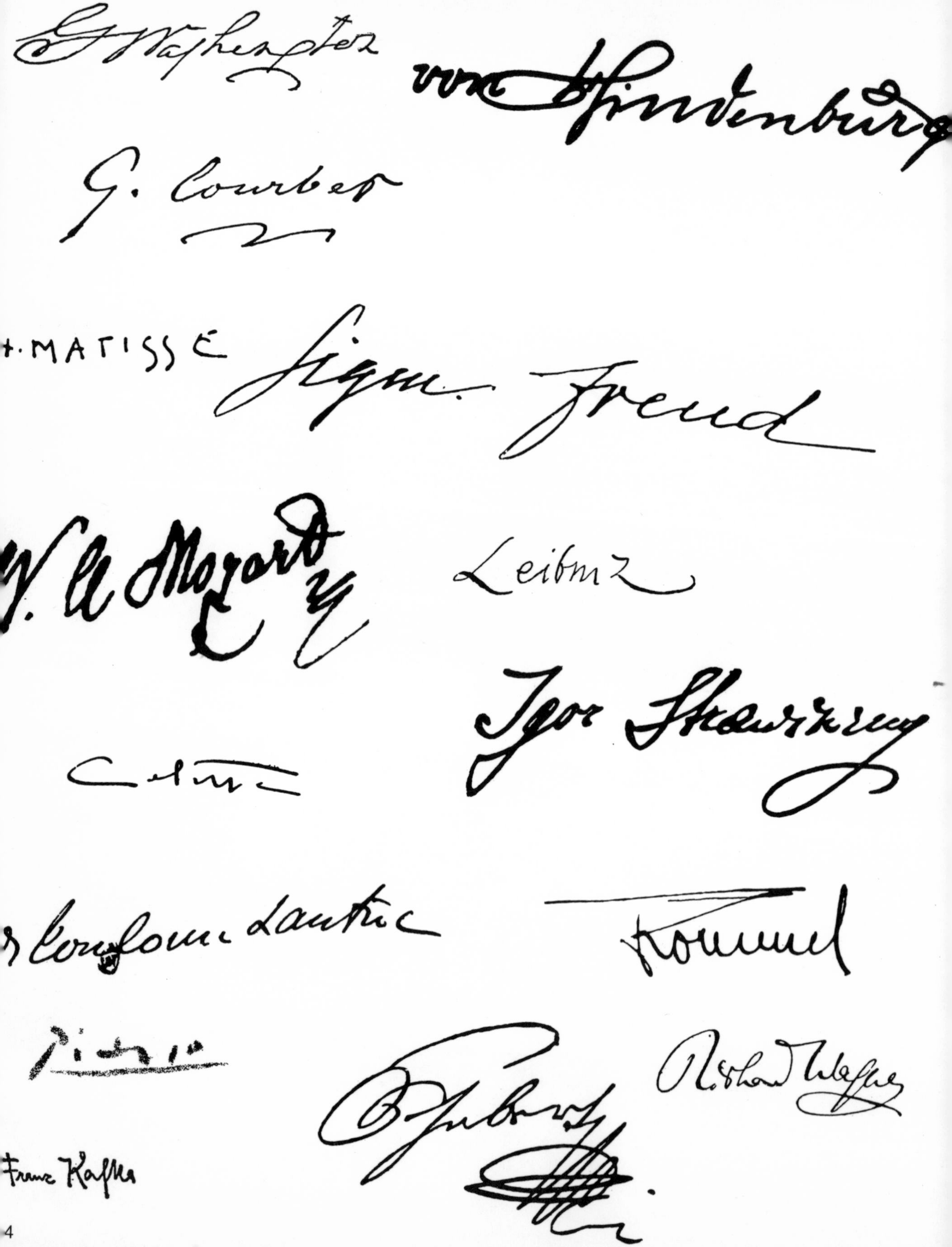
von Hindenburg
G. Courbet
MATISSE
Sigm. Freud
Igor Strawinsky
Rommel
Franz Kafka

Washington, Hindenburg, Courbet, Matisse, Freud, Mozart, Leibniz, Colette, Stravinsky, Toulouse-Lautrec, Rommel, Picasso, Schubert, Wagner, Kafka, Alexandre Dumas, Tolstoy, Prokofieff, George Sand . . . The reader may wish to exercise his skills on these extremely varied signatures.

Below, left: the signature of the painter Fujita in Japanese characters and European letters: the message is the same.

The signatures of Ludwig II of Bavaria, at different ages; on the road to madness . . .

Balzac. Below and right, two specimens of his handwriting. With thick, almost illegible strokes, he throws onto paper the output of his seething imagination. Excesses in everything – work, sleepless nights, good living, too much coffee – were no good for either his heart or his liver, as this sample of his hand strikingly shows.

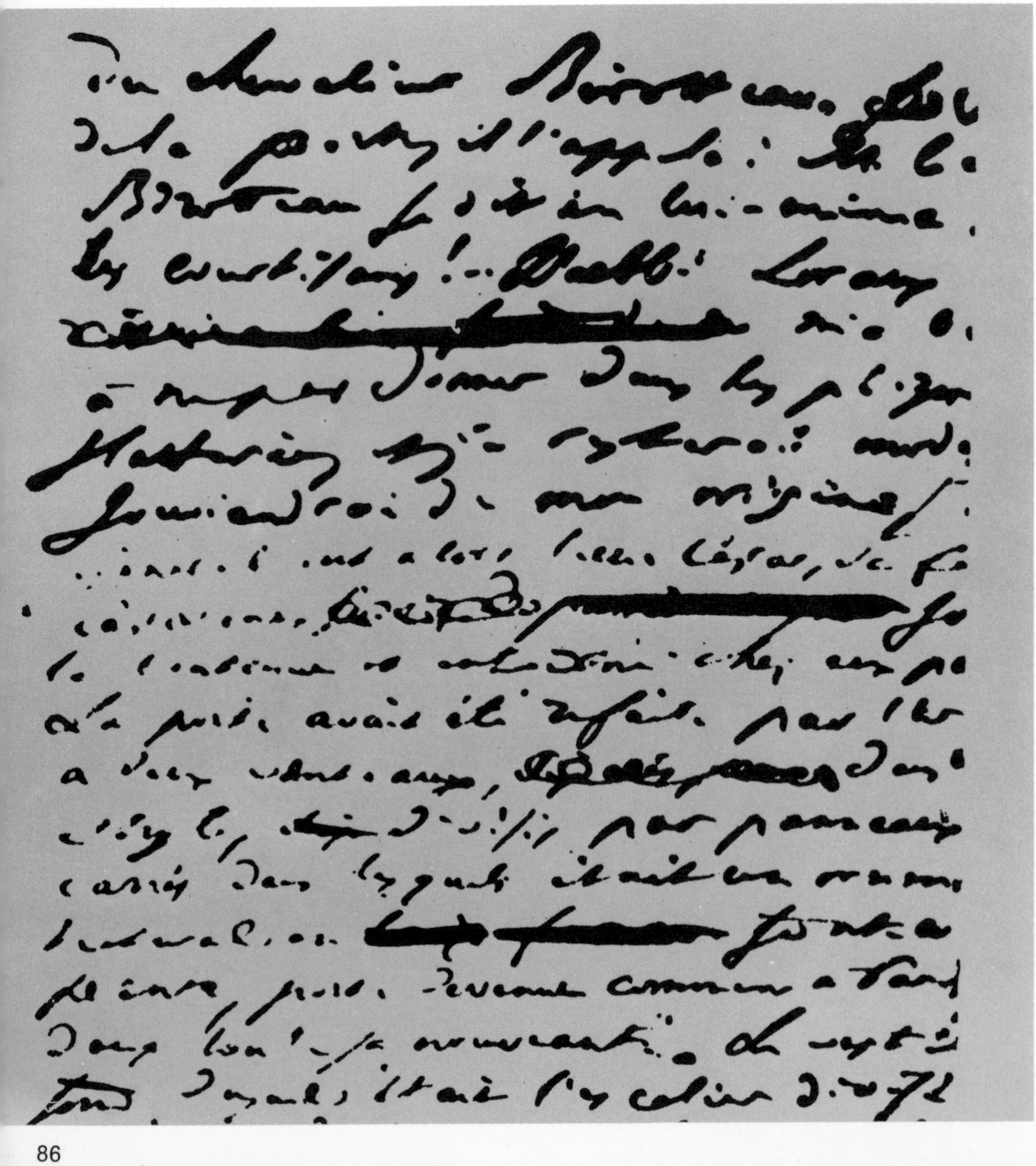

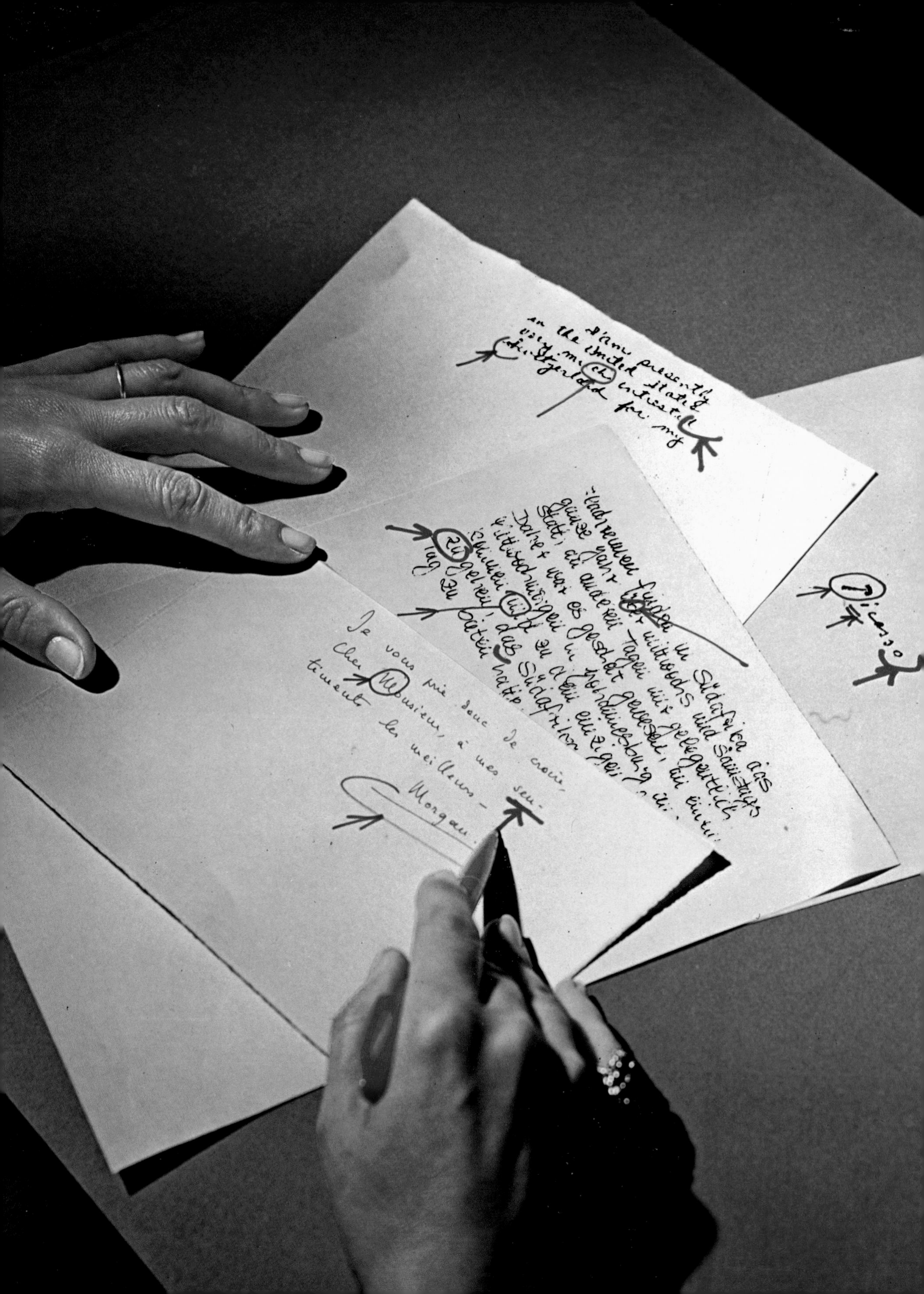
I am presently
in the United States
very much interested
Switzerland for my
Je vous prie donc de croire
Cher Monsieur, à mes sen-
timents les meilleurs
Morgan

Left: a famous signature, and three specimens of characteristic handwriting styles: Anglo-Saxon, Germanic and Latin. – Below: translation into Esperanto of a phrase written in Oriental characters. Many of the relationships still await clarification . . .

11. National Handwritings.

Latin types of handwriting.

These specimens of Latin handwriting range over a century and a half. They are the work of a writer (98/ Gustave Flaubert), a publisher (99/ Hachette), a professor or engineer (100/101), a jurist (102), and secretaries or business people (103/104).

The dominant traits are an inclination in the direction of the movement of the hand, a fast, effortless line, and a smooth linkage between the letters. Thought and sensitivity both follow their own natural course, sloping with an almost instinctive logic.

Imigination is given free rein, without ever—at least in these examples—falling into excesses. The sheer speed of association stimulates thought and invites quick repartee, witty rejoinders and an occasional word of astringent criticism.

Swept along in an impetuous movement of the pen, the writer's thoughts do not always have the time to stop and dwell in depth on a subject. In keeping with their temperament, Latins press on quickly, talk a lot and become vehemently excited, for or against something, rather than merely becoming intrested in it.

Besides the dominant traits mentioned above, one should note the rather slight incidence of angular shapes, of accentuated vertical lines, of authoritarian cross-strokes

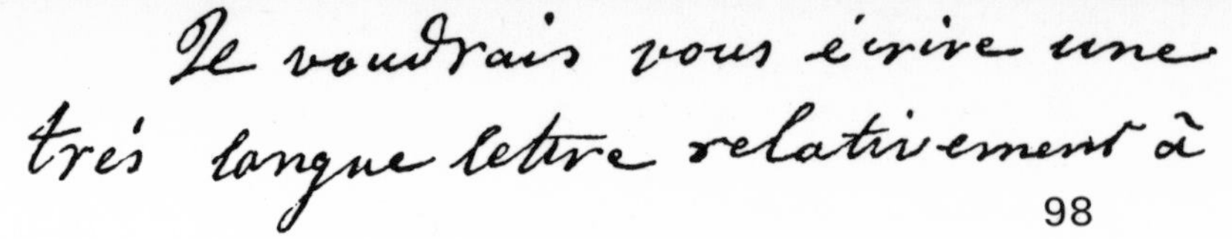

98

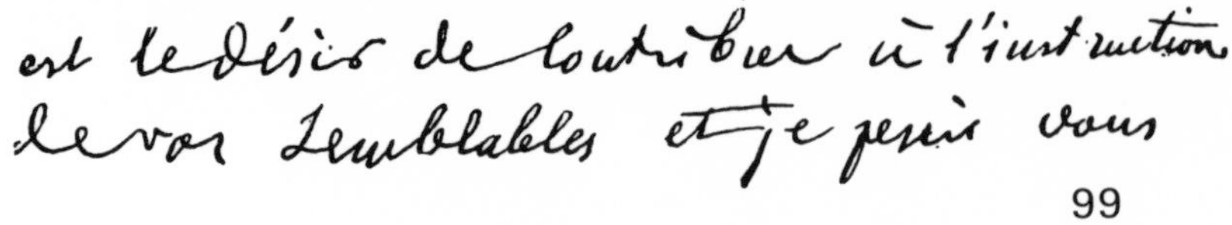

99

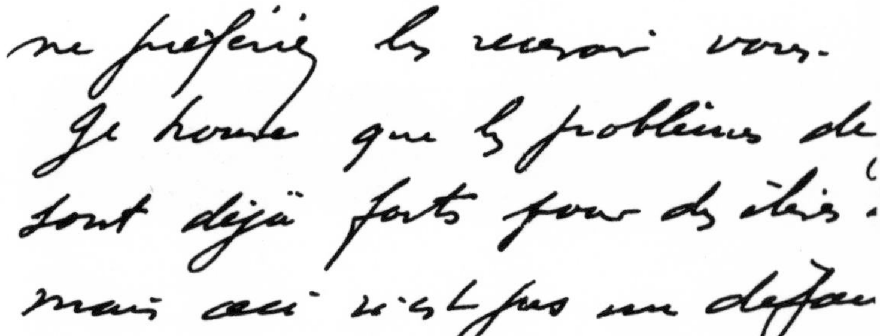

100

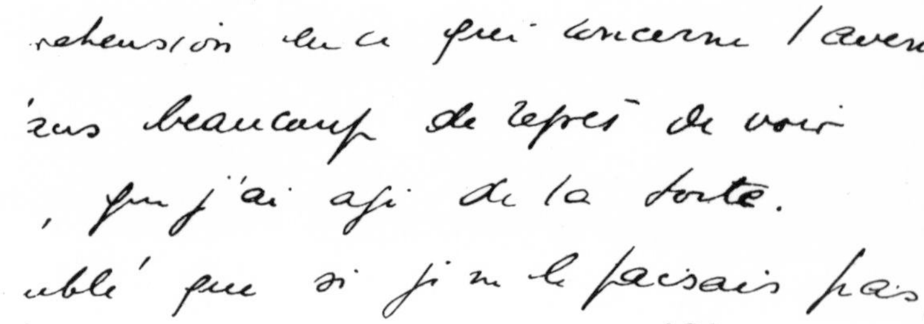

101

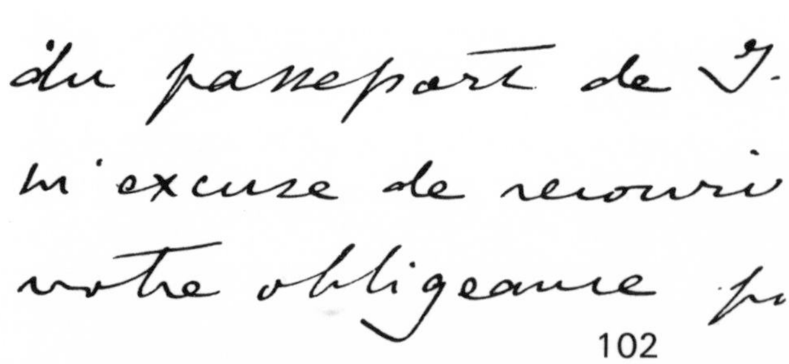

102

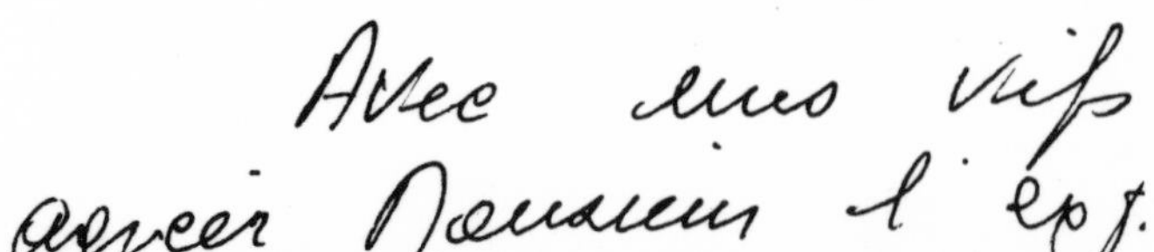

103

104

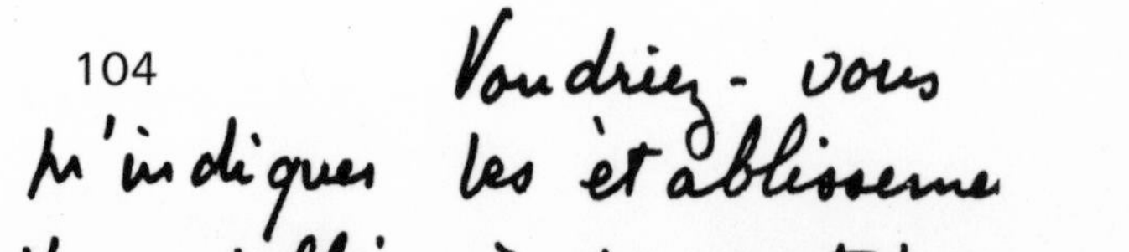

105

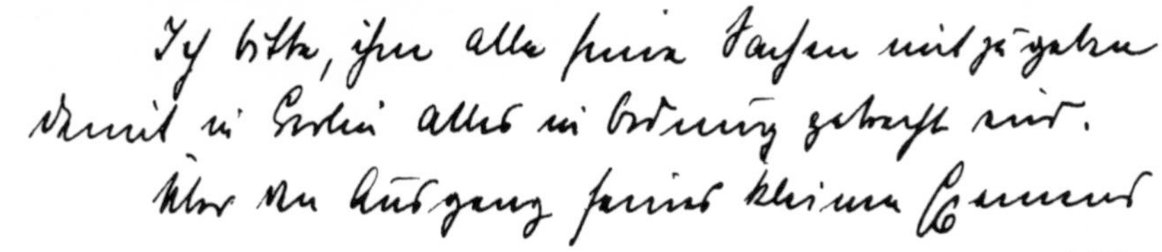

106

on the *t*s, as are commonly found in Germanic hands. The Latin type prefers flair and the barbed riposte to the harsh grind of discipline. It may be less efficient, but it is certainly amusing.

Of course, the examples given here do not reflect the Latin character, but merely give one of its many aspects. Nevertheless, the typical features are clearly discernible: clarity, casual, relaxed manner, vivacity; reason and sensitivity, neither of which are dominant; and imagination, which, in the long run, gradually gives way to realism.

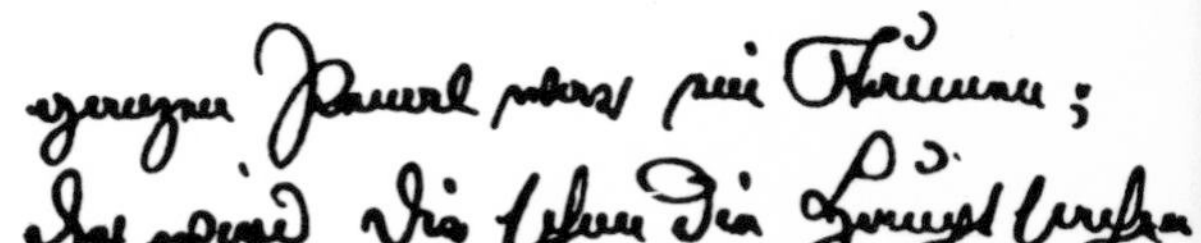

107

German handwriting

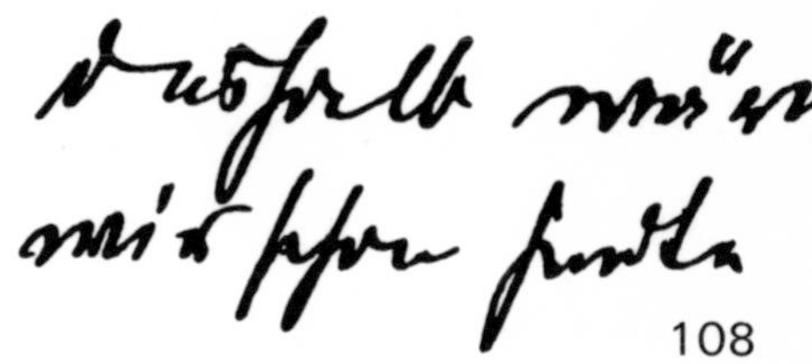

108

The main features of this type are heavily accentuated lines, and angular shapes, which speak of the desire to command and, at the same time, of obedience to discipline.

Depending on the period and the temperaments involved, this spirit of discipline will manifest itself plainly, either with blunt military hardness (105/ Bismark), or in a form somewhat softened by sensitivity (106/ diplomat).

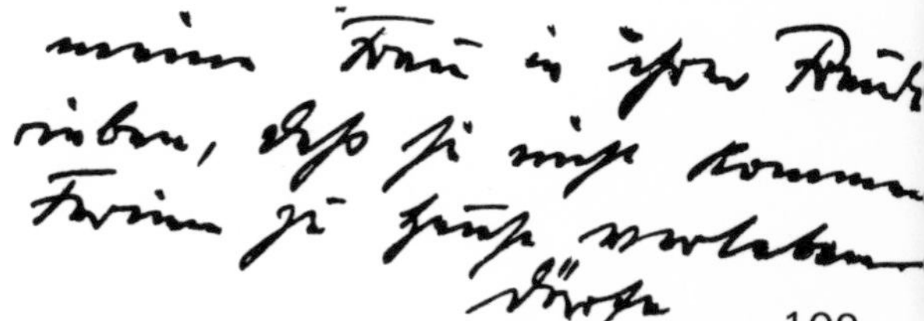

109

But in all Germanic hands, whether they be rigid Prussian, jolly Austrian or rounded Bavarian, deliberately accentuated lines predominate. From the thick pen of the poet-philosopher psychologist (107/ Lavater), to the heavy pressure and the vivacity of those who like to think of themselves as particularly virile (108/109–industrialists), the prevalent feature is the person's ego—individual or national.

Even those who try to adapt themselves to another style of handwriting and another mentality (110/111–two samples of handwriting from the same person) cannot quite

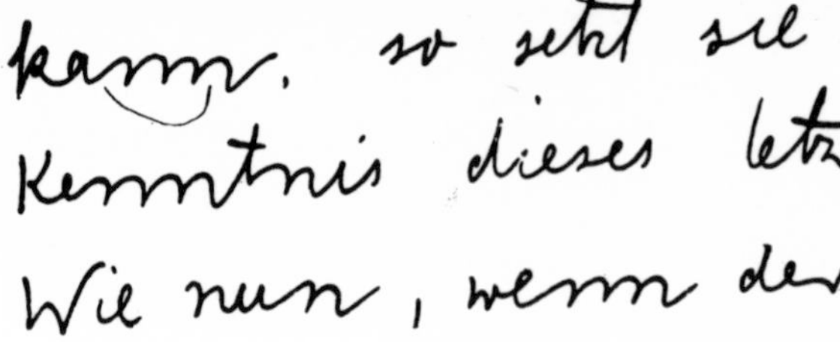

110

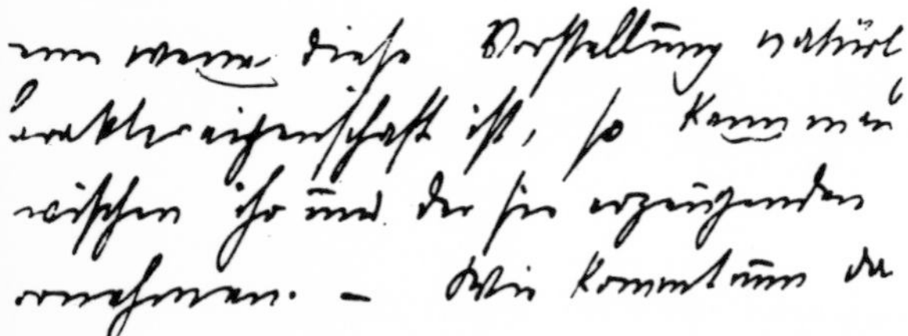

111

shake off the predominance of arched letters and angles (in this case, the letter *n*).

There is an increasing tendency, however, for Germanic handwriting to drop the jerky, sharp movements which, at one time, used to slow it down so considerably (112) Greater amounts of trade and cultural exchanges have doubtless help make this so.

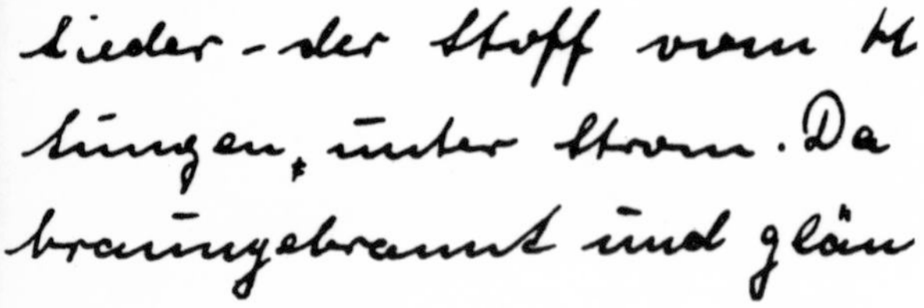

112

32 year-old woman, newspaper vendor. – Natural ability rather than acquired expertise enable this young woman to succeed in both her professional and her private life. Intelligent, sensitive, sensual, she fulfills her role as a woman with ease.
She assumes a certain coquettishness in bringing out her physical and spiritual qualities. Thus, she is rarely totally sincere.

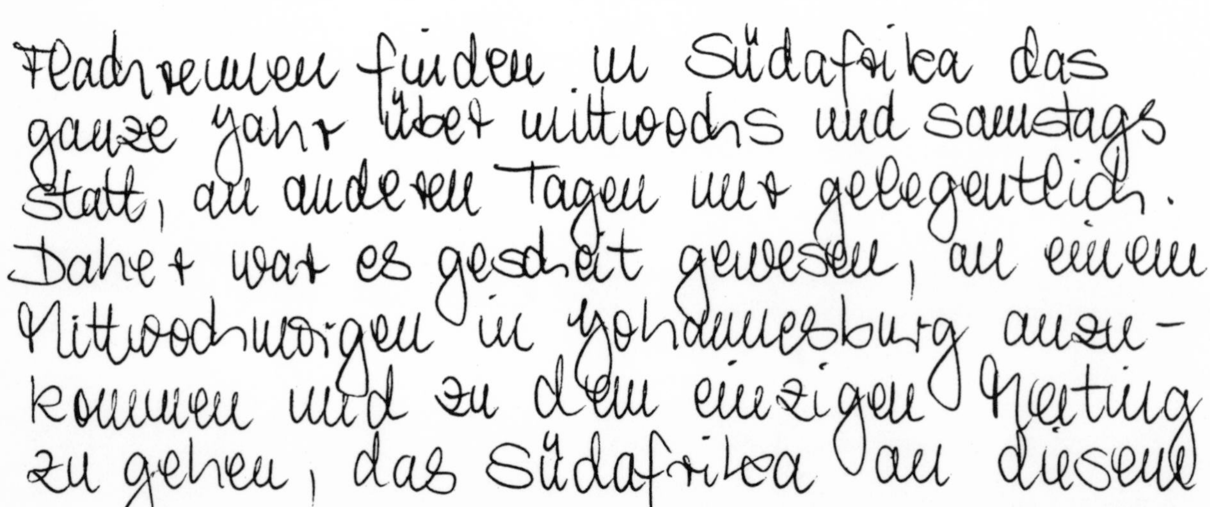

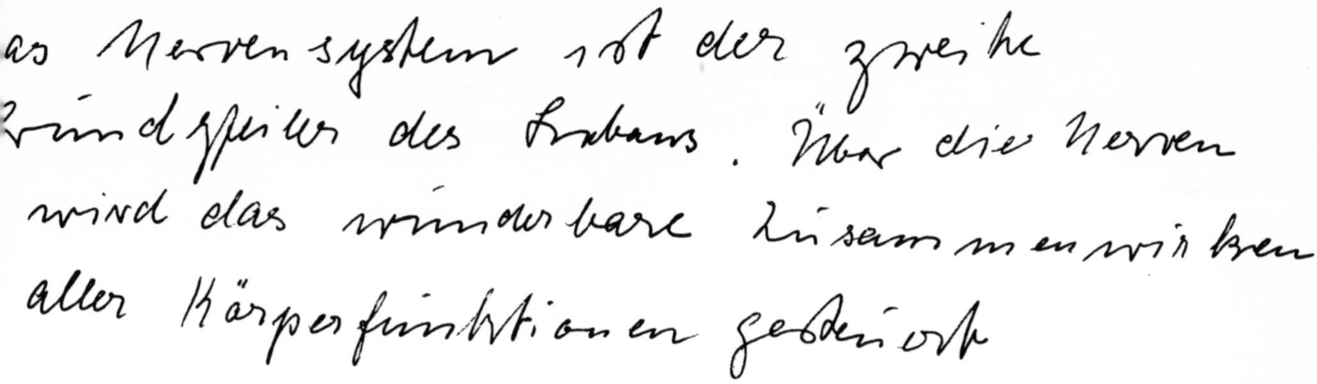

as Nervensystem ist der zweite

wird das wunderbare Zusammenwirken
aller Körperfunktionen gesteuert

62 year-old woman, no profession. – Both realistic and imaginative, she has a lively intelligence and shows a willingness to learn. She is logical in her thought and her behaviour. But generally unwilling to listen to or accept the arguments of others. She tends to be cold in her relations with other people and attaches little importance to matters of the heart.

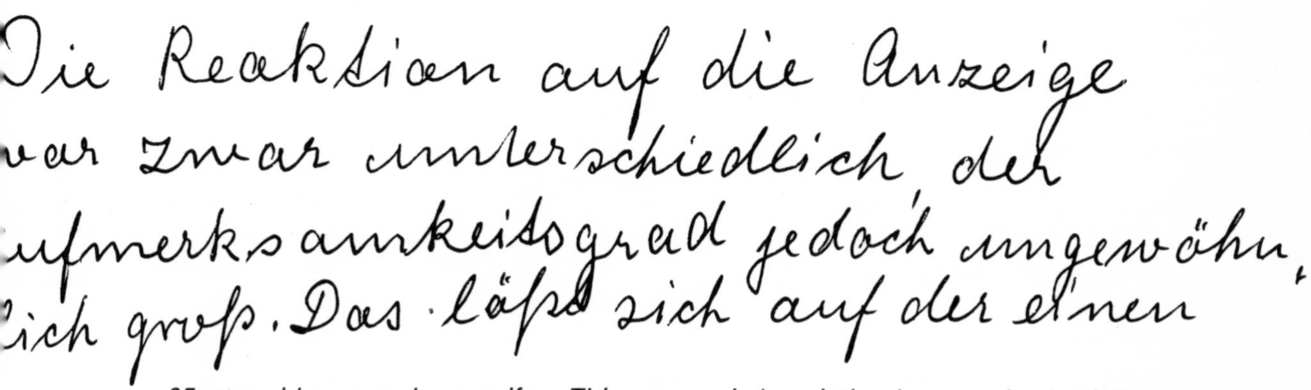

Die Reaktion auf die Anzeige
war zwar unterschiedlich, der
ufmerksamkeitsgrad jedoch ungewöhn-
lich groß. Das läßt sich auf der einen

65 year-old woman, housewife. – This woman, in her sixties, has remained childish, or relapsed into childishness. Her spirit reflects softness, gentleness, candour and confidence. Incapable of doing harm, she does not believe that others could wish to harm her. While not unintelligent she thinks and acts more with her heart than her head.

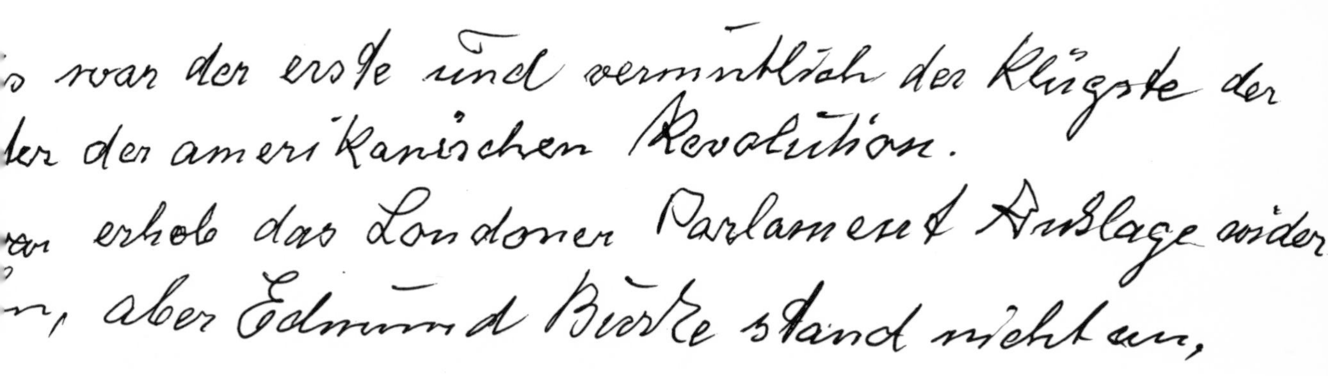

war der erste und vermutlich der klügste der
der amerikanischen Revolution.
erhob das Londoner Parlament Anklage wider
aber Edmund Burke stand nicht an,

71 year-old man, retired jockey and jazz musician. – The writing is clear and seeks to create an impression of the forcefullness of an old man whose life was marked by movement and activity. He still assiduously fulfills his daily duties. But he seems to be vulnerable to certain nervous disorders which might have repercussions on his physical health and his characterial equilibrium.

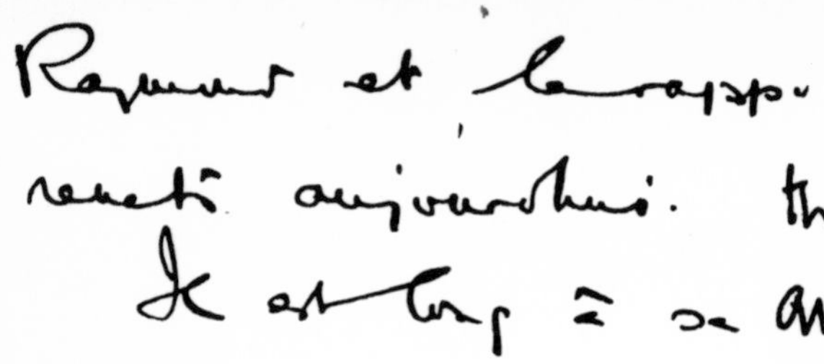

113

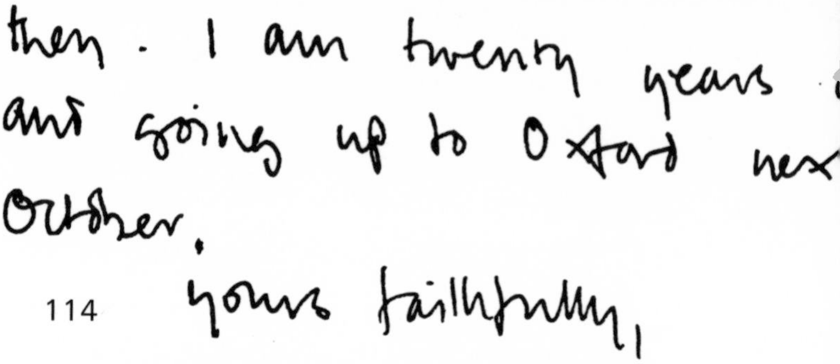

then. I am twenty years
going up to Oxford next
October.
Yours faithfully,

114

Anglo-Saxon handwriting styles

The Germanic peoples who invaded the British Isles in the 5th and 6th centuries brought with them not only their laws and customs, but also the dominant traits of the German character.

To varying degrees, therefore, Anglo-Saxon handwriting has some of the characteristics of German handwriting, particularly those relating to affirmation of will, and concrete accomplishments. This dominant trait is clearly visible in 113 (British industrialist, 40) and 114 (British student, female, 20).

On the other hand, a tendency towards angular shapes is less readily apparent. Firmness and self-discipline are shown not in the Germanic tone, but through restrained willpower, seasoned with a sense of humour and a phlegmatic approach. English handwriting is usually straight or sloping slightly to the left. Passion and sentiment are both contained. Sample 115, for instance, (Englishwoman, 40) is a good illustration of this kind of restraint, which may border on dissimulation.

In the handwriting of Americans, Anglo-Saxon features are usually to be found, though, generally speaking, in a less disciplined form. Particularly in the case of young persons (116/female Student, 20), the independent will manifests itself against a background of fairly loosely-knit character traits. Yet the forms of American handwriting are numerous. Many samples can be seen to have undergone the influence of Latin, as well as Anglo-Saxon, hands (117/art dealer; 118/writer, traveller). Beneath the diversity of forms, the free-and-easy manner, desire for independence and individualism of the average American can be discerned.

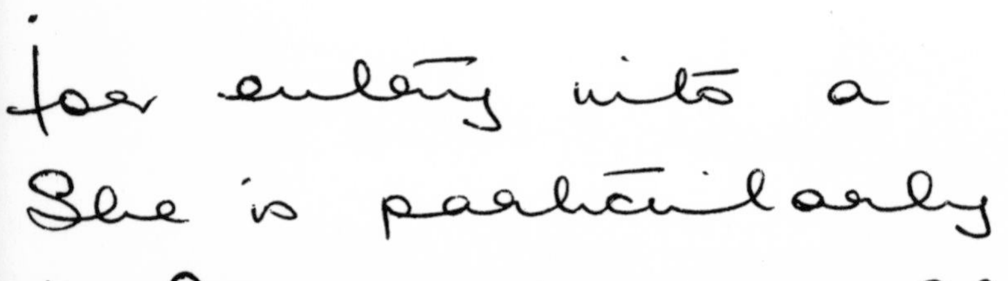

115

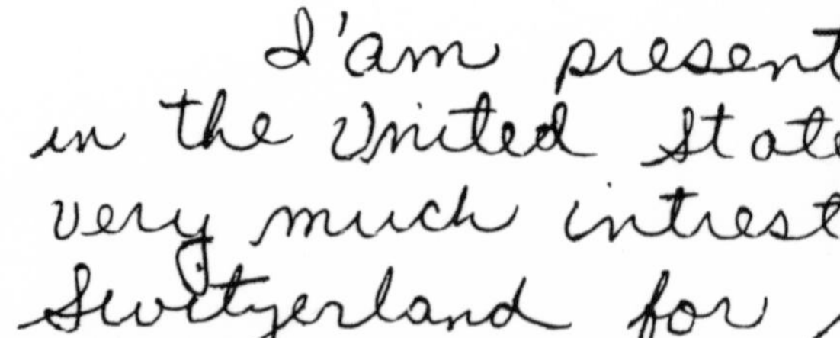

I am present
in the United State
very much interest
Switzerland for

116

117

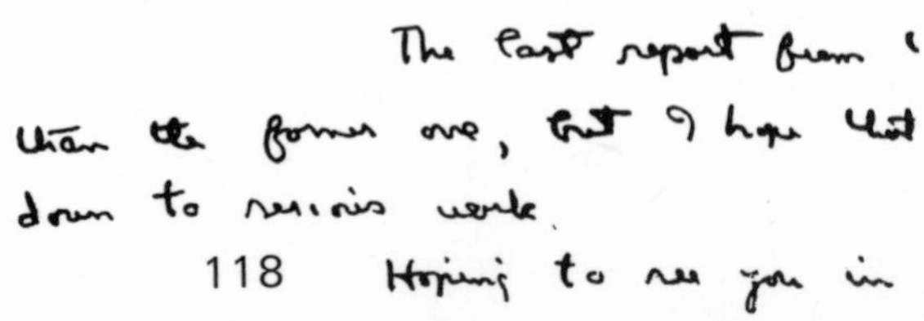

The last report from
than the former one, but I hope that
down to serious work.
Hoping to see you in

118

a bicycle passing it, your musical
companion I think of those days in
the corner ground floor rooms.
Anticipate remaining here over Christmas
and probably into spring, grinding out

English writer, 40. – A subtle analytical mind, well served by an intuition and a sensitivity which enable him to deal with subjects in both the arts and the sciences. He is a simple, candid and sociable person, and thus enjoys the respect of his peers, despite his sometimes irritating nervousness.

I have something belonging to you - too
big for me - black and rainproof.
Just checking on your present or
change of address. Mine :

American photographer, female, 30. – Both professionally and in her private life, realism and technique come before sensitivity and sentiment. This very confident young woman, with an almost manly temperament, does not allow herself to be influenced by either the suggestions or the orders of other people. She goes her own way, following her own ideal and her own ideas; but she goes in a straight line.

moment. Lovely
country, bright but freezing
weather.
All good wishes from

English teacher, 45. – She is not indifferent to things of the senses, and he is able to strike the right kind of balance between the pleasures of the body and the satisfactions of the mind. Although he is English, it is unlikely that he has much of a sense of humour.

by himself & is very nice but he is
too old for her 38 (so she thinks) & she is not
very keen on him. Another thing about it
is he is divorced (he is the innocent party)
& has three little boys. I wish she
could find a nice young fellow about
two or three years older than herself but
it seems hopeless here at the moment.

English woman, 65. – She is not lacking in sensitivity, though she applies a studied discretion to her emotional life. She is a practical woman, with plenty of common sense, though she sometimes finds herself devoting much more attention to a variety of pet projects than to immediate accomplishments. While not without ideals, she nevertheless appreciates material satisfactions.

and music, with in fact a guilty conscience, as I felt
you should have these by now!
If by any chance (and it now
seems unlikely) I can call at Geneva on the
way home also, I'll ring you at U.N, but I doubt

English teacher, 40. – A lively mind, illuminated by an intuitive imagination which sometimes causes it to depart from traditional logic. He is skilled in analytical and synthetic thought, but with scant regard to the kind of order which his teaching subjects should require. His sensitivity and human qualities are real enough, though they are somewhat spoilt by a bit of agitation.

enjoy yourselves there. You will only b
seven miles from here, so we will be
at hand if you need anything.
The Baptist Minister is back from Switzerl

Irish woman, 60. – A good woman; she is always very active, either in support of or against something. She is restless, talks a great deal and is simultaneously anxious that others should need her, and confident that they do. She applies herself to this purpose wholeheartedly, even though her frankness occasionally leads her into an indiscretion.

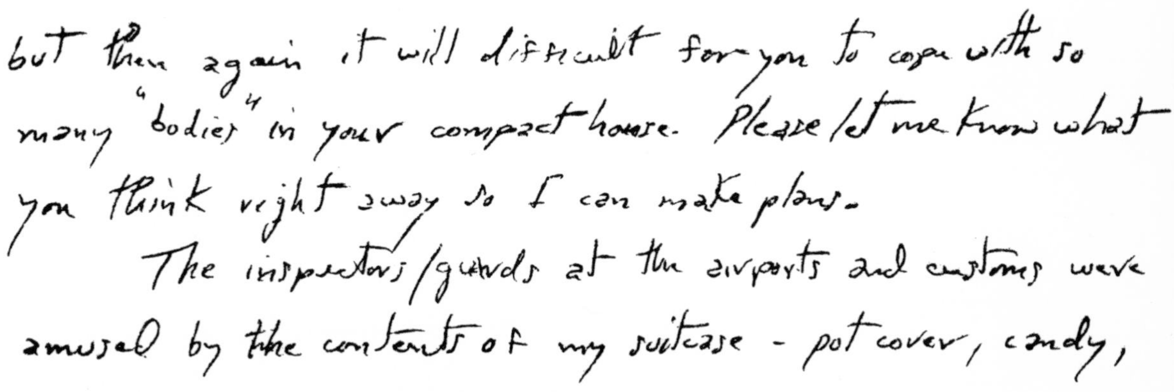
but then again it will difficult for you to cope with so many "bodies" in your compact house. Please let me know what you think right away so I can make plans.
The inspectors/guards at the airports and customs were amused by the contents of my suitcase - pot cover, candy,

Director – Computer Corporation, USA. Both physically and mentally, this man lives on his nerves. If his thoughts and acts were not sustained by a solid professional ability and a sense of order, they would quite probably degenerate into paradoxes and fantasies. He constantly seeks to maintain his own sense of order so as to honor his professional and family commitments. Being very demanding on himself, he is entitled to make demands on others.

Handwriting is becoming internationalized.

In the three types of handwriting—Latin, Germanic, Anglo-Saxon—it will be noticed that handwriting tends more and more to shed a variety of details and subtle distinctions which usually slow it down, and to conform increasingly to the physical demands of technique.

The typewriter, machines which print one's thoughts and transmit them to some remote corner of the world have had the effect, to some extent, of programming man's body, soul, and character in a certain direction.

One has really to examine the signature in order to find specific character traits still intact. The signature and its accompanying flourishes are not under the influence of the environment; they instinctively express the preferences and real nature of the individual.

With the growth of the communication media, trade, and the ideological and political inter-penetration of states, nations and races, the basic distinctive features peculiar to each of them have begun to become somewhat blurred. Travel, international business deals, international congresses and conferences, are all having a levelling effect on both character and handwriting, with the result that, fairly soon, only the signature will convey the true nature of a hand.

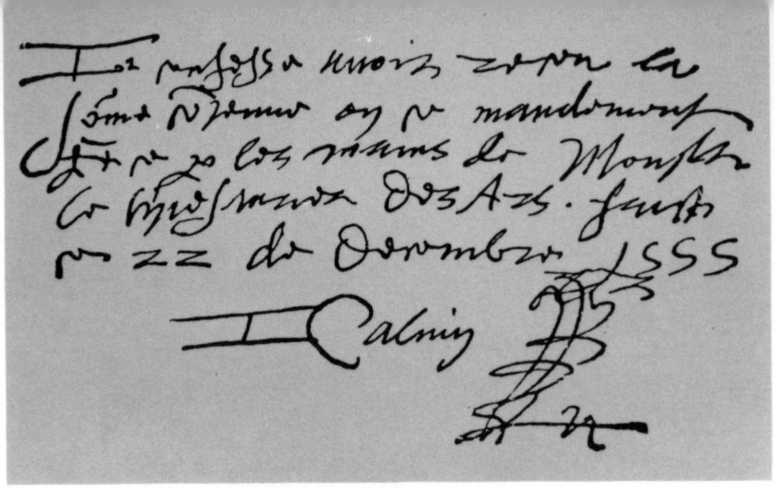

12. Relationships between character and handwriting.

SIGNS OF GENERAL SUPERIORITY.
(intelligence, morality and will)

PSYCHOLOGICAL SIGNS	GRAPHOLOGICAL SIGNS
Activity	Fast, rising, simplified hand; cross-strokes on *t* placed forward; acute accent changed to grave accent in French; accents connected to the next letters; joined words.
Sensitivity	Hand of uneven size, shape and direction. Letters and words and lines of uneven size, shape and direction; light hand, with letters formed separately within words.
Simplicity	Simple, natural, spontaneous hand.
Moderation	Sober, moderately inclined hand, lacking in big movements; lines slightly rising, not too uneven; lines markedly rising, followed by others which tend to be more or less horizontal.
Distinction	Absence of common traits, signs indicating art, taste, order, simplicity; light hand.

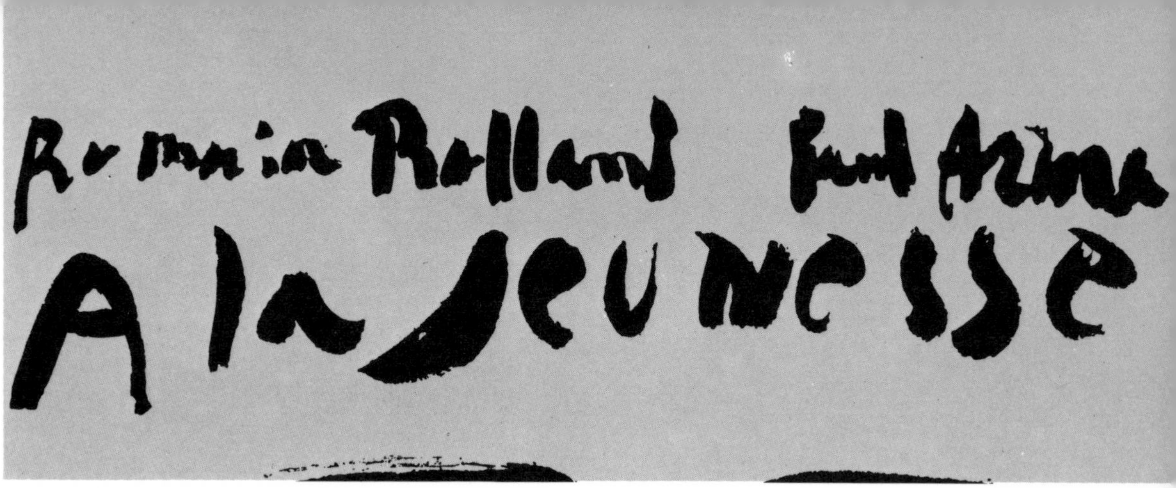

SIGNS OF GENERAL INFERIORITY

(intelligence, morality and will)

PSYCHOLOGICAL SIGNS	GRAPHOLOGICAL SIGNS
Inactivity	Curves too emphatic; slow, dropping hand; round hand; cross-strokes on *t* missing.
Lack of sensitivity	Straight, even monotonous hand.
Lack of simplicity	Exaggerated, eccentric, pretentious letters.
Passion	Broad sweep of the pen; sharply sloping hand, signs of excitement.
Vulgarity	Common traits, exaggerated shapes, absurd ornaments.

Below, left page: five lines by Calvin, and his signature. The angles and hooks of this tormented hand are evidence of the severity which the Reformer showed towards himself and others. His style radiates lively thinking, a prodigious capacity for hard work, and closely linked reason and faith – but not warmth, or serenity. Above: handwriting by Picasso, who seems to use his pen as a brush, whether he is painting or writing. A dynamic and transparent graphic style, written by a confident hand, using strokes full of life and colour. Here, words speak the same language as the lips and the eyes.

SPECIAL SIGNS OF INTELLECTUAL SUPERIORITY

PSYCHOLOGICAL SIGNS	GRAPHOLOGICAL SIGNS
Well-ordered imagination	Big, harmonious, confident movements of the pen; big hand.
Thoughtfulness	Sober hand, judicious, careful punctuation.
Clarity of ideas	Tidy, legible hand; words and lines well spaced out.
Flexibility of ideas	Curved, wavy hand.

SIGNS OF MORAL SUPERIORITY

PSYCHOLOGICAL SIGNS	GRAPHOLOGICAL SIGNS
Rectitude	Letters and words of equal height; lines straight; regular, simple hand.
Altruism	Capitals joined to the following letter, final letters written from left to right, *n* and *m* formed like *u*, sloping hand, *e* written like a French circumflex accent

SIGNS OF SUPERIOR WILL

PSYCHOLOGICAL SIGNS	GRAPHOLOGICAL SIGNS
Constancy	Handwriting and cross-stroke on *t* even and regular; firm, dynamic hand.
Energy	Firm and slightly angular hand, straight and clean, not very fine; cross-strokes on *t* and underlinings heavy emphasized; no hesitation in direction of lines.

SPECIAL SIGNS OF INTELLECTUAL INFERIORITY

PSYCHOLOGICAL SIGNS	GRAPHOLOGICAL SIGNS
Disorderly imagination, or no imagination at all	Big, uncertain movements of the pen; inharmonious enlargement of small handwriting.
Thoughtlessness	Agitated hand, big movements of the pen; words, letters and accents omitted.
Confusion	Words and lines blurred; untidy hand.
Stubbornness	Angular, regular and rigid hand; cross-strokes on *t* forming acute angle.

SIGNS OF MORAL INFERIORITY

PSYCHOLOGICAL SIGNS	GRAPHOLOGICAL SIGNS
Lack of rectitude	Wavy lines; confused handwriting; thread-like words; lack of simplicity.
Selfishness	Reverse hooks on capitals and final letters; cramped, angular hand; signature flourishes spiral or wedge-shaped.

SIGNS OF INFERIOR WILL

PSYCHOLOGICAL SIGNS	GRAPHOLOGICAL SIGNS
Lack of constancy	Handwriting irregular and uneven; cross-strokes on *t* sometimes missing; rounded hand.
Weakness	Fine, wavy hand, with exaggerated curves; cross-strokes on *t* thin or missing; lack of firmness in the stroke.

Assorted examples for study.

Cervantes

Cervantes

The illustrious Cervantes has a masterly handwriting. Just consider for a moment the incredibly imaginative and lively flourish which accompanies his signature! One can almost imagine Don Quixote swept away by a windmill and dumped on the ground 20 feet further on! (fig. 119).

Unconnected letters: strength of intuition, sense of observation.

The breadth of the capitals shows his confidence in his own strength.

Notice some odd features: the small *g* is cut in two by an inharmonious connection to the next letter. These very few words by the great Spanish writer convey a most compelling impression of energy and gaiety.

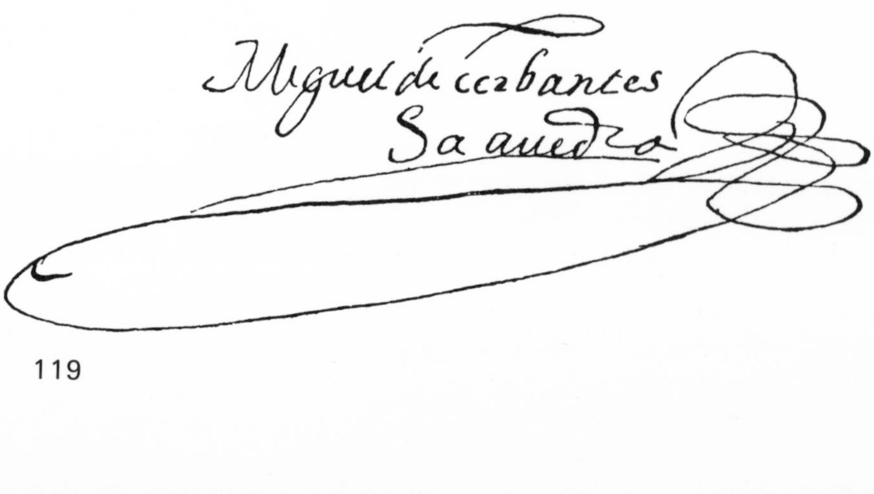

119

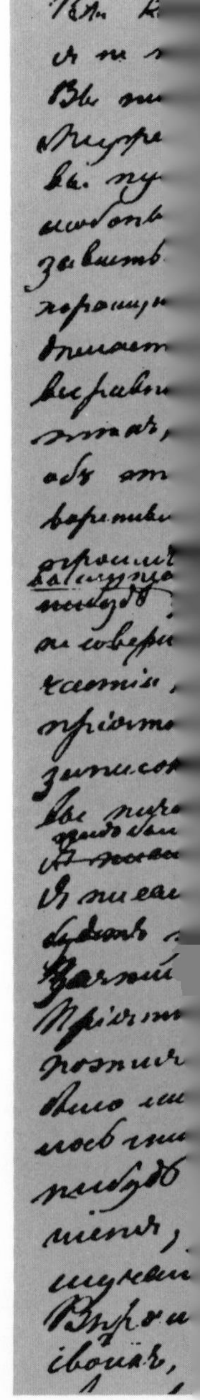

Tolstoy

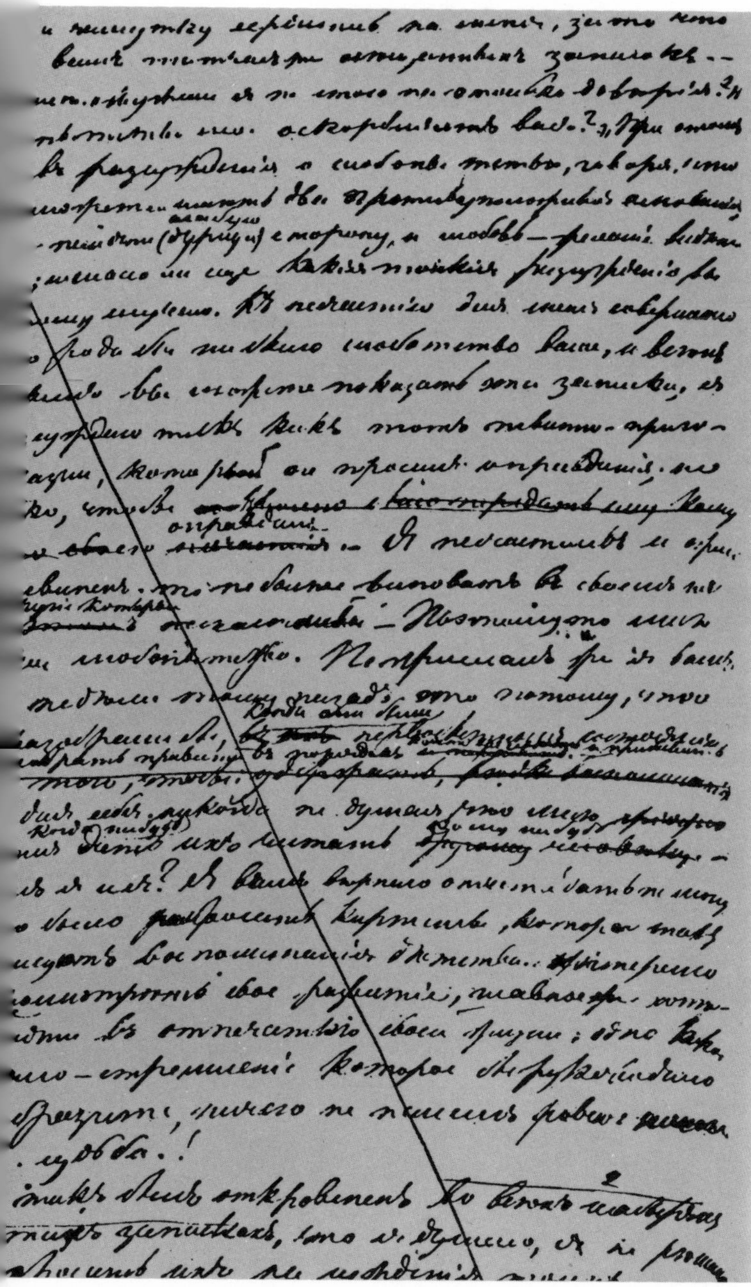

Tolstoy

This page, from one of Tolstoy's early manuscripts, does not really lend itself to a graphological analysis of the author's whole personality. It is probably from the period of his military service, which, apart from the normal soldierly duties, was a time of youthful excesses and high spirits (fig. 120).

The artist and the poet are certainly visible in this rather small handwriting, which is both studied and brisk, sensitive and sensuous; it is, however, difficult to discern the idealist, the moralist and the disciple of Christ, who would rid himself of all his possessions, and give them to those who have nothing.

The blurred letters, the heavy erasures and superimposed corrections, letters thickened almost to the point of illegibility (particularly towards the bottom of the page), all combine to present a distinctly earthy image of the author, who was then in his thirties.

However, signs of Tolstoy's later concern with things of the spirit do appear in certain lighter forms and more exhaustive features to be found in his handwriting. The sweeping shafts, the openness of the buckled letters, the rounded style, almost completely lacking in angles or hooks, give us a glimpse of his special brand of genius, which was of a moral and spiritual nature.

Tolstoy loved hard work, and was virtually obsessed by the job of regenerating the world; these are traits of his character which are already discernible in the closely-packed handwriting which fills this page, and which indicates his desire to suppress nothing that his conscience requires him to say.

121

Shelley

This brief sample of Shelley's handwriting conveys an impression of independence of mind and action, and of passionate and lyrical expression. The speed and lack of restraint and discipline in the formation of the letters do not preclude a certain ethereal elegance and grace, and do not make it particularly difficult to read (fig. 121).

This brisk hand obviously belongs to a man with strong surges of poetic feeling, while, at the same time, it speaks of Shelley's love of independence and the unselfish ardor with which he rebelled against all forms of tyranny and sought to escape from their control.

However, the relaxed free-flowing style of the young poet-pamphleteer with the impetuous sweep of its final letters, is also characterized by letters of unequal size and shape, and uneven spacing.

A very pronounced sword-shape—the words Yours, Percy, Shelley—suggests a lack of sincerity on the part of the poet, if not in his literary work, at least in his subversive pamphlets and fiery polemics.

The small hooks which come at the ends of words are not a sign of objectivity and disinterestedness. The long, slender line beneath the signature—as pointed as a stylus—seems to suggest that, besides being a brilliant and distinguished poet, Shelley also had an excellent, incisive command of prose.

Shelley

Livingstone

Livingstone

This big, firm hand conveys the dominant traits of Livingstone's character: will-power and generosity. The explorer and the missionary—his dual nature—were well served by these forces which moved his mind and his heart respectively (fig. 122).

By temperament, Livingstone was passionately involved in the great problems of nature and life, whether the sources of the Nile or the condition of the black people.

The energy which emanates from this very full hand, with its moderate inclinations, fairly continuous liaisons, a hand which, despite certain clumsy formations, is clear and easy to read, transmits a powerful, living image of the man who, for more than thirty years, travelled around southern Africa as a missionary and an explorer.

The fact that most of the letters are linked together, and the generally rounded style of the hand are evidence of the strength and mobility of an independent mind. The high, thick cross-stroke of the *t* confirms this desire for independence of action, which served Livingstone as an active defense to any obstacle to the free affirmation of his thoughts and feelings.

But Livingstone does not always seem to have responded to the demands of his excessively rich temperament by bringing a prudent critical spirit to bear on them. He was so carried away by the firmness of his beliefs that his impulsive nature and his passions often led him into error and disorder. The dots on his *i*s are either missing altogether or in the form of an almost casual dash. As he was swept along by his imagination, and heeded instinct more than reason, Livingstone failed as a scientist in his quest for the source of the Nile. The force of his generous heart enabled him to free the Blacks from slavery. One more than makes up for the other.

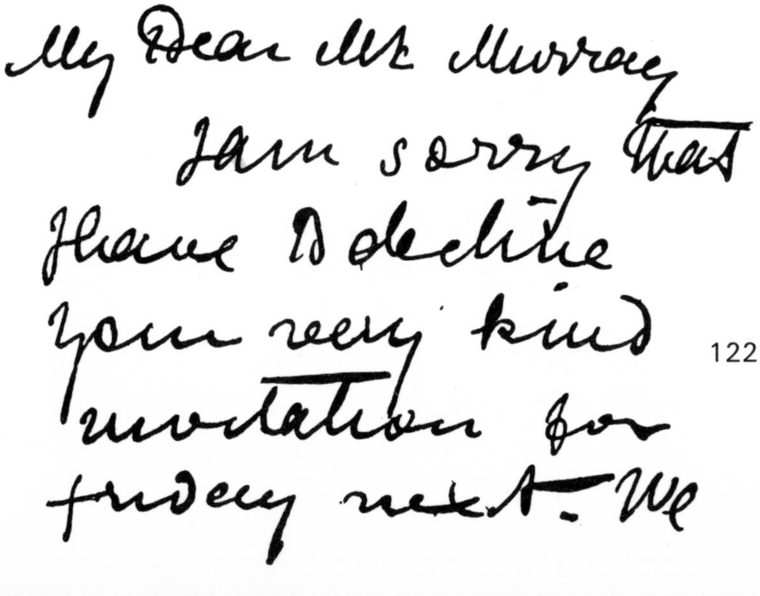

My Dear Mr Murray
I am sorry that
I have to decline
your very kind
invitation for
Friday next. We

122

Edison

Edison

It would be difficult to find the slightest trace of sensitivity in this square, almost print-like handwriting by Thomas Edison. The lines are straight, while the letters all seem to be glued down to an invisible base; these traits, together with the deliberate slowness, in general, of this pre-eminently tidy hand, are the mark of a man with great technical gifts, rather than delicate reactions to art and human concerns in general (fig. 123).

How does one explain these enormously long cross-strokes on the *t*'s, which seem to have been written with a ruler, and which cover entire words at a time? And what about the huge cross-stroke on the *T* of his name? They lack both the power of an unbridled imagination and the strength of authoritative will-power; rather, they are evidence of steady self-control, used to protect the inventor's ideas and accomplishments. The only thing that speaks of the power of Edison's ideas, and of his determination to get them across, is the huge, clubbed bar which sweeps over his entire signature.

We are indebted to Edison for inventions which have played a prime role in modern progress. But were they all the result of his gift for discovery? Signs of creative imagination are so conspicuously absent from this hand that one is inclined to doubt this was so.

On the other hand, Edison excelled at giving concrete form to the inventions of others, by imparting to them his practical sense, his gifts as an observer, and his powers of analysis and synthesis. At all times, he proved able to extract from his numerous associates the greatest measure of efficiency, by himself setting the example of a methodical mind, firmness of character and an endless capacity for hard work.

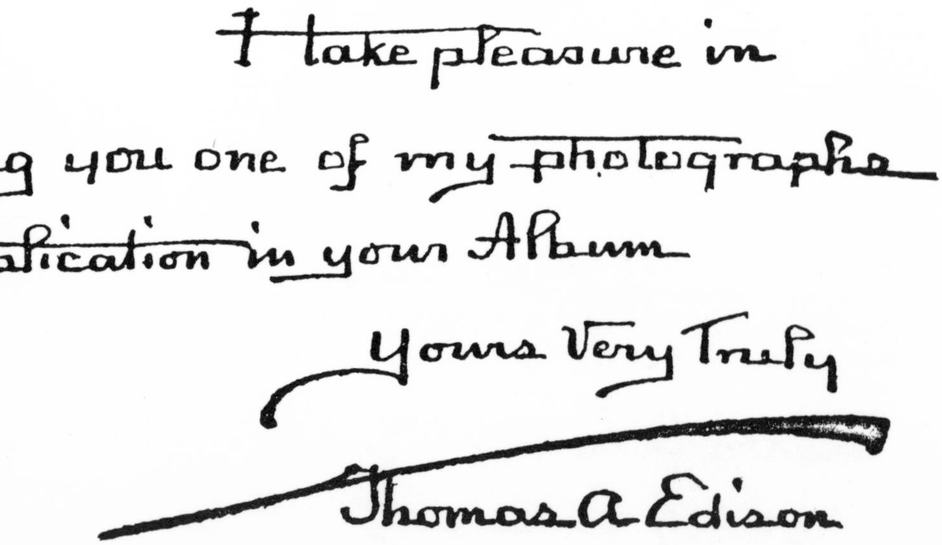

I take pleasure in
sending you one of my photographs
for publication in your Album
Yours Very Truly
Thomas A Edison

123

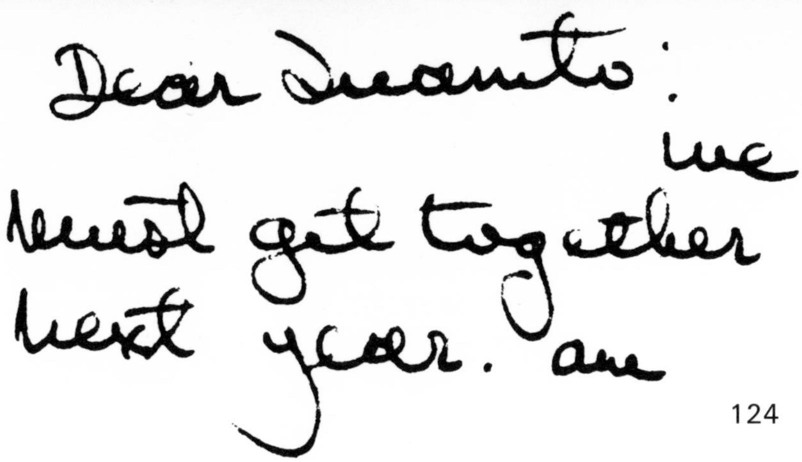

124

Hemingway

"Man was not made for defeat. A man can be destroyed, but he can't be defeated." Hemingway said these words passionately: and he acted according to them, with equal passion, throughout his life (fig. 124).

Yet, does his handwriting speak this kind of language? It appears to be a perfectly plain, transparent expression of his rich personality, as seen through its ample, generous proportions and simplicity of line.

However, the thickness of his strokes, the heavy, swollen nature of certain letters, and the descending lines all combine to give the impression that Hemingway felt dominated by disorders which had long been threatening him: hypertension, arterio-sclerosis resulting from the serious injuries which he had received during a life-time of adventure. The breaks which can be observed at the top of certain shafts and other looped letters show that he is really deeply disturbed:

This hand does not, therefore, say much about his innermost thoughts, nor about the subtleties of his sensitive personality. But certain traits, such as the speed at which it seems to have been written, the fact that some final letters are rounded and also end in a slight flourish, and, particularly, the cross-strokes on the *t*s, reveal the author's stubborn affirmation of his strength in the face of adversity, and his determination to overcome evil.

One might say *certainty*, as well as *determination*. The looped *t*, with the cross-stroke before, after or above the loop, the nature of the joins between the letters are evidence of Hemingway's unspoken anxiety about sickness and death. This is an anxiety which dated from the end of the First World War, when the discovery of his own mortality depressed him so severely, and which was now going to overwhelm his gradually declining physical and nervous strength. This specimen of his handwriting is a prelude to that decline.

Hemingway

Faulkner

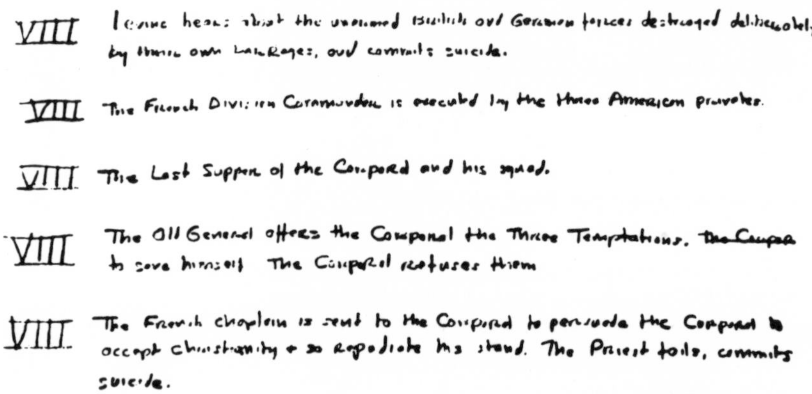

VIII Levine hears that the unarmed British and German forces destroyed deliberately by their own barrages, and commits suicide.

VIII The French Division Commander is executed by the three American privates.

VIII The Last Supper of the Corporal and his squad.

VIII The Old General offers the Corporal the Three Temptations. ~~the Corporal~~ to save himself. The Corporal refuses them

VIII The French chaplain is sent to the Corporal to persuade the Corporal to accept Christianity & so repudiate his stand. The Priest fails, commits suicide.

125

Faulkner

This minute hand is the work of Faulkner, when writing the outline of his "Parable", a Christian allegory which was so full of ambition and noble sentiments as to pose a daunting challenge for the reader (fig. 125).

The charge of "unreadable" was levelled against Faulkner's work by many critics. However, with close scrutiny, it is possible to get a clearer picture of the thinking and motives of the writer. At first, this seems to be the handwriting of an analyst having the acute powers of observation of an entomologist, who draws exactly what he sees, whether from real life or his imagination, in the finest detail.

Although it seems stereotyped, and severely limited by its sheer smallness, this hand nonetheless reveals an intense inner life. It is an intense, introverted hand, one in which emotion, sensitivity and imagination surface but rarely from the great depths at which they function. This style is entirely without lyrical flourishes: rather, it embodies a contained passion, a sobriety and a discretion bordering on timidity. Faulkner was clearly no man to admit others readily to his private life.

It is true that his handwriting was not always like this. Earlier manuscripts are written in a larger hand, more open and more relaxed. But in this specimen, written about the age of 55, the author's thoughts seem to be withdrawing into themselves, to be moving away from the living images on which it had formerly been based, and sinking into abstraction and symbols, illegibility and confusion. Even so, the forceful cross-strokes which are found in this specimen express the novelist's firm determination to find language to embody his profound and solitary experience.

126

Goethe

This sample contains just two words and a signature, yet it fully conveys the dominant traits of Goethe's character. The sharply sloping style, enormous down-strokes, and a touch which, while generally light, has a sensuous force about it at certain points, all belong to a man whose passions are expressed otherwise than through ideas and sentiments (fig. 126).

Instinct, intuition and intelligence are all intermingled in the genius who was responsible for the creation of "Faust". Yet his imagination, sensitivitiy and fiery temperament also make him a lyric poet, vehement and tumultuous in his early years, and later more obedient towards the classic rules of the spirit and the heart. The words in the illustration, in which Goethe proclaims himself to be a "very obedient servant", are certainly from this period.

The small letters seem to be huddled together, out of obedience to the dictates of reason.

But the final hook of the signature brings us back from the sphere of the spirit and of sentiment to that of material things and the senses. Right up till his declining years, the poet was firmly and passionately anchored in that world.

His tumultuous temperament manifested itself in areas other than his poetry and drama. Goethe certainly did not disdain the good life, nor material blessings. Just like his Faust, he must have found himself signing little pacts with the Devil on more than one occasion . . . The broad, sensual sweep of his signature show how fully he gave himself to life, in body and soul.

Goethe

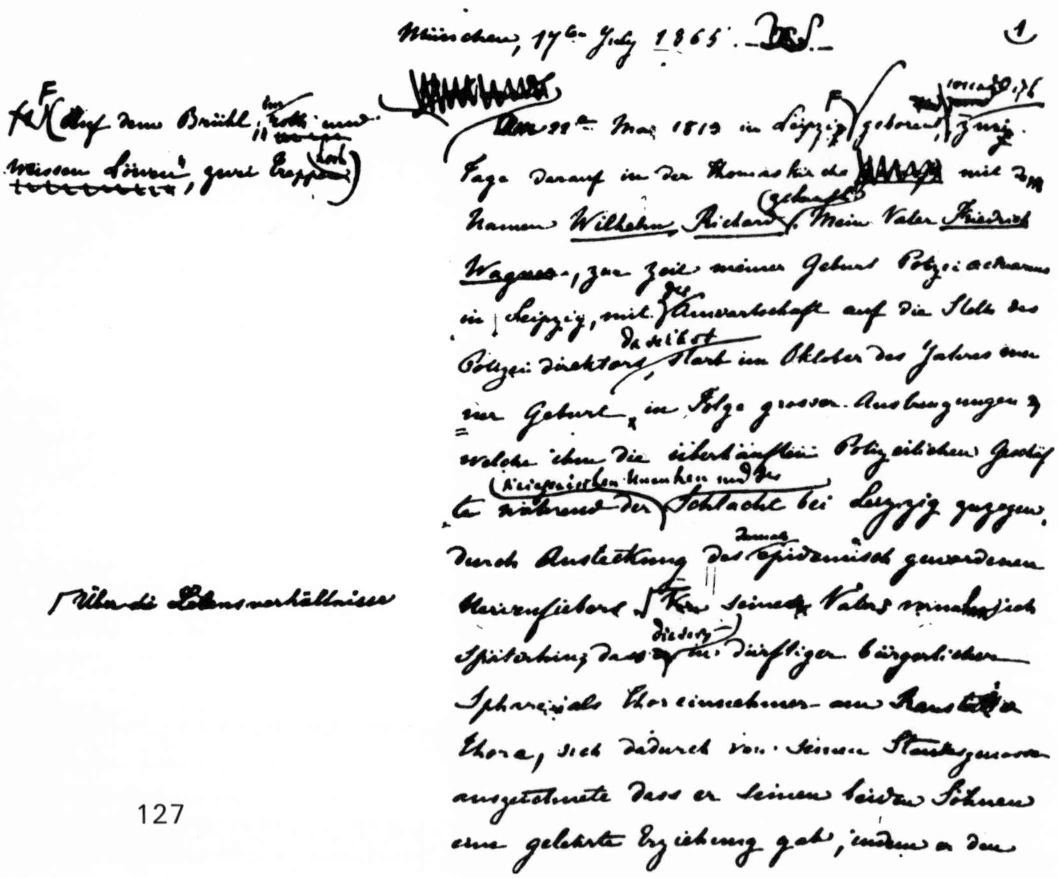

127

Wagner

This first page from the manuscript of Wagner's Memoires was written in 1865; the composer was 52 at the time, and felt a pressing need for a new clarity and a new order in his life. Accordingly, this specimen reflects just one phase of his turbulent life, a period of relative calm (fig. 127).

It is somewhat surprising to find nothing in this handwriting which expresses the grand romantic style of Wagner's music. This tiny, cramped hand, with numerous erasures and super-imposed corrections, would appear to leave little room for powerful surges of emotion and imagination.

Yet, even though it is cramped, it is, nonetheless, not static. It is clearly driven along by strong passions, up or down, as the case may be. However, this passion is dominated more by the senses than by the spirit, as can be seen from the dominant—and very down-to-earth—vertical strokes.

The really striking feature of this manuscript page is the disturbed "ego" which emerges from it. Although this is a lively hand, firmly written, it is laced throughout with egocentric movements and distinctly low punctuation, the signifiance of which is emphasized by the author's habit of curving downwards at the end of certain lines.

If it is true to say that Wagner's artistic achievements were, above all, dramatic, it is because they reflect his whole personality, which was thoroughly impregnated with the dramatic spirit.

Does this manuscript mark the end of the pessimistic period in Wagner's life? One year after he wrote these lines, he was to enter the period of peace and happiness provided for him by Cosima Liszt, and which enabled him to complete his creative endeavors. His handwriting was certain to become more serene as a result.

Wagner

Freud

Freud and psychoanalysis both have their ardent supporters and their merciless critics. What are we to infer about the personality of the great psychologist from this short specimen of his handwriting? (fig. 128).

Here we have a man who is clearly dedicated to research and the quest for knowledge, a man who exercises his intuitive genius in a feverish attempt to discover the how and the why of the tangible phenomena of consciousness. It is a fast, partly angular hand, uneven, linked, slightly descending, often quite blurred; this is the handwriting of a scientist, who, by virtue or his temperament, is more drawn towards the depths of the soul, than towards the pinnacles of the mind.

Although the rapid style of this hand reflects an intelligence which is superior on account of its lucidity and power of penetration, the heaviness and the blurring of the line at certain points could be said to explain, in a sense, the sexual aspect which Freud sees in all problems before him. Wasn't this obsession with sexuality a phenomenon of a morbid origin in Freud?

The fact that instinctive tendencies predominate over spiritual forces in Freud's handwriting helps us understand better his passionate preference for studies of psychic instinct and animal nature, as compared to the higher forms of human thought.

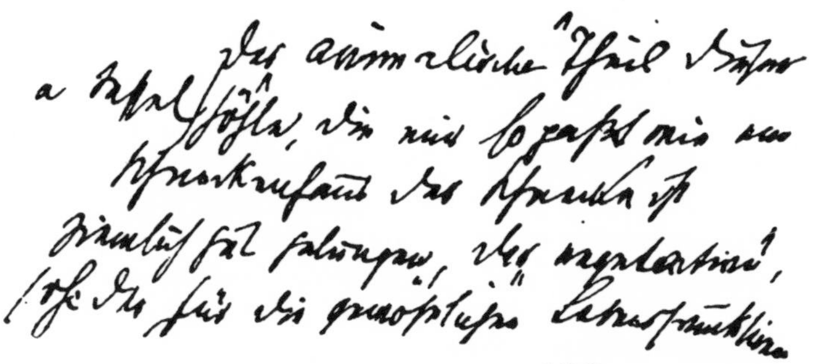

128

Freud

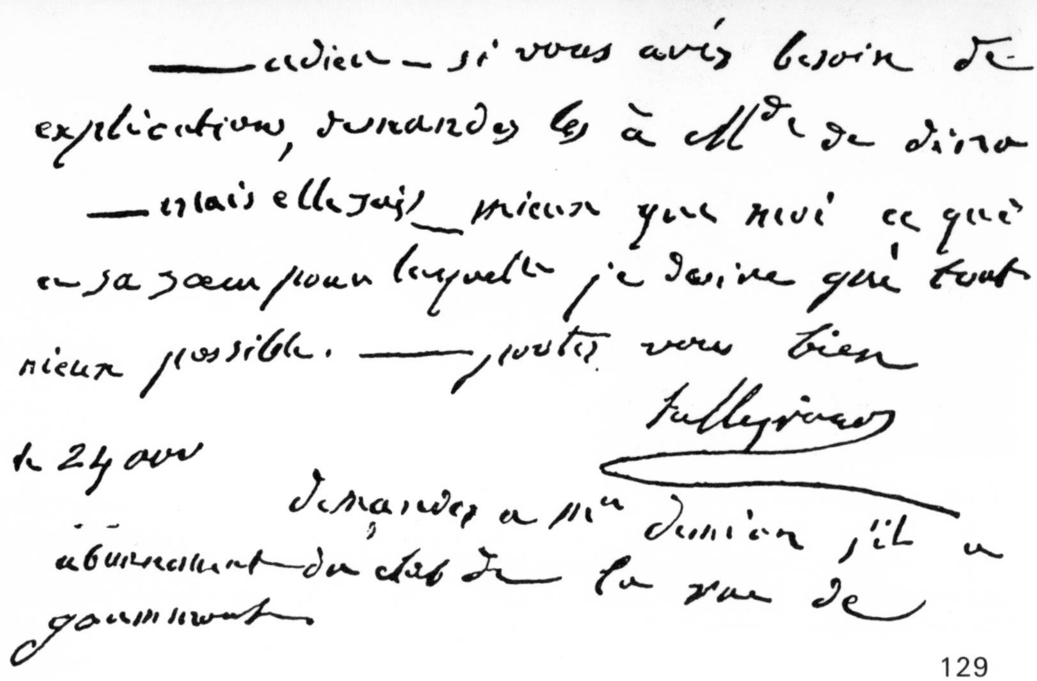

129

Talleyrand

Talleyrand firmly believed that writing should be avoided wherever possible; and there is much to be said for such a principle. As the Latin tag goes: *Verba volant, scripta manent*, "spoken words fly away, but written words remain". Without this letter, which is a masterpiece of diplomatic writing, history would never have known how thoroughly devious and mean this major figure of the late 18th century could actually be (fig. 129).

1. This is a rising hand, therefore the work of an ambitious person. All lines, except the last three, follow a rising line, denoting intense powers of concentration, perseverance and the ability to follow difficult negotiations through to the end with a complete disregard for any obstacles he may encounter in the process.

2. This man, who had been born sensitive—as can be seen from his signature—is constantly forcing his letters into an upright position. In each word, one can discern a curious struggle between two instincts: the natural and the artificial. As soon as Talleyrand forgets his official nature, the writing suddenly slopes and becomes sensitive. Just look at the last word, *Grammont*. Despite all his cleverness, it would never have occurred to Talleyrand that we would have chosen to examine such a word to find out that there was still some heart in him.

It is this inner struggle, in this handwriting and others like it, which gives the curiously heavy and boxlike shape which is due to the perpetual mixture of the horizontal and the vertical letter.

This is a man who constantly seeks to ensure that his true self will remain invisible and impenetrable.

3. He avoids capitals, anything like a sweeping movement in the formation of his letters, and, in general, anything suggestive of imagination, poetry, intellectual greatness, or the flowering of generous or beautiful notions in the soul. The letters are dry, dead, close together: the important thing is to avoid saying too much. Man was given the gift of speech in order to disguise his thoughts; it follows, therefore, that handwriting must serve the same purpose. In keeping with this theory, handwriting must contain nothing that does not perform some function. The proper names which he has occasion to quote are no exception: all are reduced to the level of small letters, including his own signature, which he makes as tiny as possible, and with a small *t*. Yet, he finds it possible to indulge the word *Madame*, by giving the initial M of the abbre-

Talleyrand

viation a capital M.

The snake can slip through much more easily and surreptitiously without the distraction of capital letters.

4. Those with devious habits of mind instinctively use the official's final stroke. Lawyers habitually avoid leaving blanks, in case the pen of some clever forger inserts a word, a figure, a *no*, a *not*, which might alter the meaning of the document. They never begin a new line without ending the previous line with a stroke which serves precisely this purpose and which they often use between sentences also.

5. Periods and commas are kept strictly in their place in this letter, which deals with fairly mundane domestic matters, exactly as if it was a *note verbale* between two Great Powers.

It is interesting to note that, having inadvertently left a small space towards the end of the letter, between the words *elle sait* and *mieux que moi*, he later decided to insert a hyphen to show that these words were meant to form a single sentence.

At all times, his guiding principle was caution: nothing was to be left to chance.

6. Here we have a man with a will of iron, which he somehow manages to hide. In diplomacy, it is essential to give the impression of being extremely conciliatory. The small *t*s are crossed very low down, some of them hardly at all. Nowhere is there an impulsive line which might suggest to the reader that he is stubborn and intransigent: that would spoil everything. Only one letter is heavily crossed; this must have been an oversight. Even Talleyrand was not perfect.

7. He is greedy and mean. He never indulges in the luxury of long endings; his pen seems to be moved by a spirit of economy.

8. Lastly, let us examine the tortuous progression of his lines. Some have a barely perceptible and almost invariable movement—the snake gliding unnoticed through the grass; while others, in places, suddenly become quite jerky, reflecting a sudden upswing in his affairs. On other occasions, a single leap expresses a complete reversal of position—after which our wily statesman goes on his way, calmly, as if nothing had happened.

Such is our analysis of this superb manuscript. In every detail, it is calculated *not* to arouse suspicion. Despite his rank, Talleyrand's signature is quite plain, deliberately so, in fact; it is accompanied by a flourish which could almost be said to make him disappear into thin air.

Though greedy, hard and, in appearance, quite commonplace, this man, with his clumsy and totally inharmonious handwriting, was nonetheless a genius. Many of his small *d*s have a hook, signifying a nasty personality, a savagely selfish person. Yet some of them have the simplicity which is characteristic of great men of great intelligence.

His letters, which are arranged in close sequence, like print, are evidence of an astonishing capacity for conceptual thought and penetrating observation. Here was a man who used to chisel his thoughts, like a master craftsman.

Delacroix and Victor Hugo

Delacroix

Victor Hugo

A hard, nervous, angular hand (fig. 130).

Not a very out-going character.

At first, a somewhat rising hand: ambitious, a desire for success.

Occasionally descending: melancholy.

Very powerful will, great energy; a domineering personality (note the cross-strokes on the *t*s).

A masterly signature: artistic aristocracy.

Unsettled form of letters means imagination, inventive powers; the rigidity of a leader of a sect.

130

This sample of Hugo's handwriting, taken from one of his poems, dates from quite early in his career, at a time when he was still full of the spontaneity of youth. It is apparent that this passage was not written with any particular application, with the result that we can reach the true Hugo through its features (fig. 131).

The striking thing about Victor Hugo's handwriting is its expression of his ability to chisel his ideas into poetic form. As can be seen from this sample, each letter is, as it were, a separate tap with the chisel. It is highly unusual for two or, still less, three of his letters to be linked together. This is the classic sign of spontaneous thinking, which quickly grasps the various aspects of a situation and exercises the highest form of intuition on it.

Such conceptual powers nevertheless have an inherent flaw, which accompanies them like a shadow: despite their aptitude for inspired guesswork, they perform poorly when it comes to logical deductions. These are men of vision, whether it be in poetry, science, invention or in industry; dialectic skills are almost completely unknown to them.

Note the splendid capital H which begins the word *Hugo*. It is a grand, masterly letter, but it is inharmonious, because the two downstrokes which form it are too far apart. If they had had the opposite defect, that is, if they had been too close, almost joined together, the sign would have indicated a shy, inhibited personality. Here, they are spread out, in a broad, leisurely style—the sign of great self-satisfaction, and the joyful contemplation of one's own spiritual accomplishments.

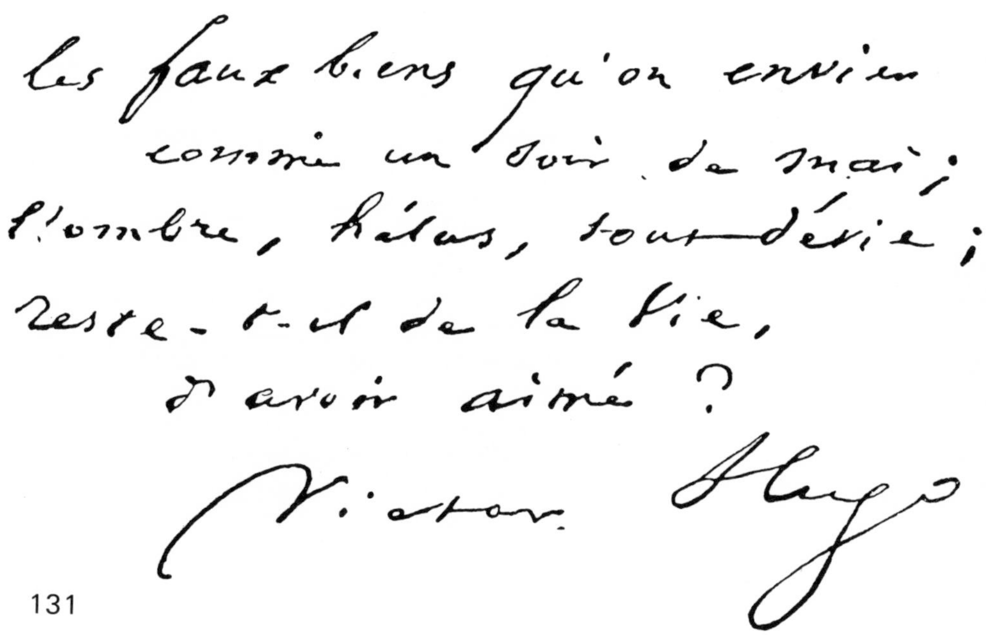
les faux biens qu'on envie
comme un soir de mai;
l'ombre, hélas, tout dévie;
reste-t-il de la vie,
d'avoir aimé?
Victor Hugo

131

Pygmalion devient l'amant
De la Vénus dont il fut père.

Victor Hugo is a Pygmalion, a powerful sculptor. It is natural that he should contemplate his work admiringly; his handwriting tells us clearly about this aspect of his character.

Hugo's imagination was very highly developed; in his handwriting it takes the form of extreme departures from the norm (The capital V of Victor, for example: the connection preceding the letter is longer than the letter itself, while the small *g* in *Hugo* is inordinately large – both phenomena being classic signs of a powerful, excessive imagination).

Yet this imagination, which soars beyond its limits, is offset by a simple view of the world, which reduces everything to the rules governing the simple and the beautiful (the small *d*s are the classic sign of this precious quality which makes for a superior intelligence; they entirely lack the scrolls which are so beloved of common men).

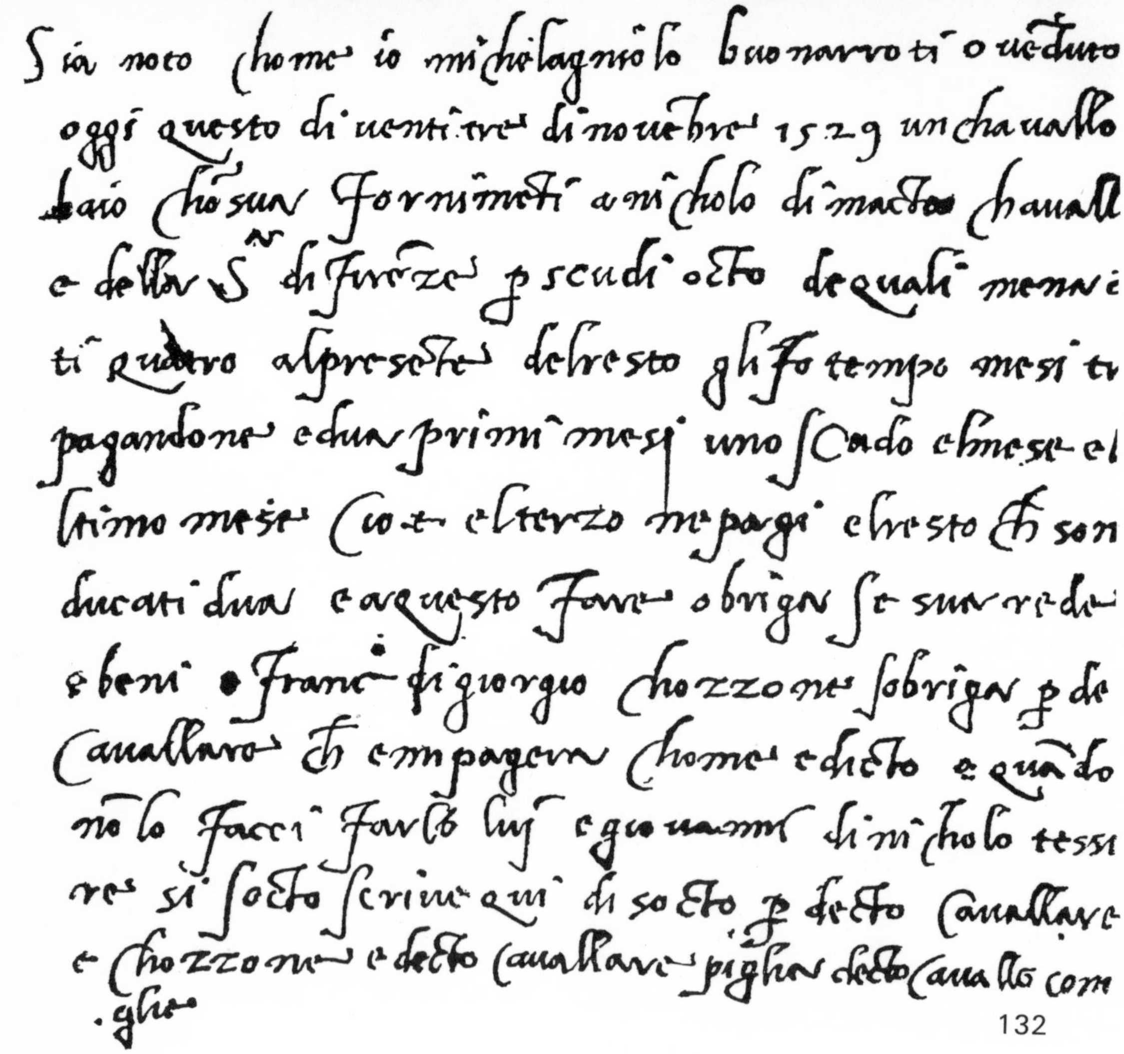
Sia noto chome io michelagniolo buonarroti o venduto
oggi questo di ventitre di novebre 1529 un chavallo
baio cho suo fornimenti a nicholo di macteo chavall
e dello S[r] di Firenze p scudi octo de quali me nne à
ti quattro al presente del resto gli fo tempo mesi tr
pagandone e d'una primi mesi uno scudo el mese e l
ultimo mese Cio e el terzo me pagi el resto ch sono
ducati dua e a questo Forne obrigo se sua rede
e beni e Franc di giorgio chozzone s'obrigo p decto
Cavallaro ch e mme pagera chome e decto e quando
no lo facci farlo luj e giovanni di nicholo tessi
tore si socto scrive qui di socto p decto Cavallare
e Chozzone e decto Cavallare piglia decto cavallo com
glio

132

Michelangelo

This document, written by Michelangelo, dates from 1529; the artist, who died at the age of 89, was thus at the height of his powers (fig. 132).

The first impression this sample creates is one of great energy; it has a fullness about it which almost makes it stand out in relief on the paper. It is clearly the work of a firm, sensitive hand, and suggests the depth of the feeling which succeeded in wresting from a solid marble block the robust, muscular shapes which are so characteristic of Michelangelo's art, and which are also found in his painting, for example, in the gigantic frescoes on the Book of Genesis, where the dramatic effect is greatly heightened by the pronounced relief which he imparts to the muscles.

This hand contains more than evidence of the artist's ability to work supremely well with his materials. Besides his sheer strength of will, and the surge of impetuous passions, we can readily discern the moderating force of reason.

This is a handwriting which could almost be said to be built in space. It is no exaggeration to say that it enables us to reach out with a finger and touch Michelangelo's creative genius as a builder. After all, this same fondness for vigorous shapes and the grand scale appear time and time again in his architecture, its finest manifestation being the dome of Peter's.

Other features of this powerful hand, such as the graceful style and the rounded shapes, speak of the artist's emotional capacities and the sensitivity which he put into certain forms of expression. Let us not forget that he was also a poet: here again, the traits of the sculpture can be discerned even in his rhymes.

Michelangelo and Verdi

Verdi

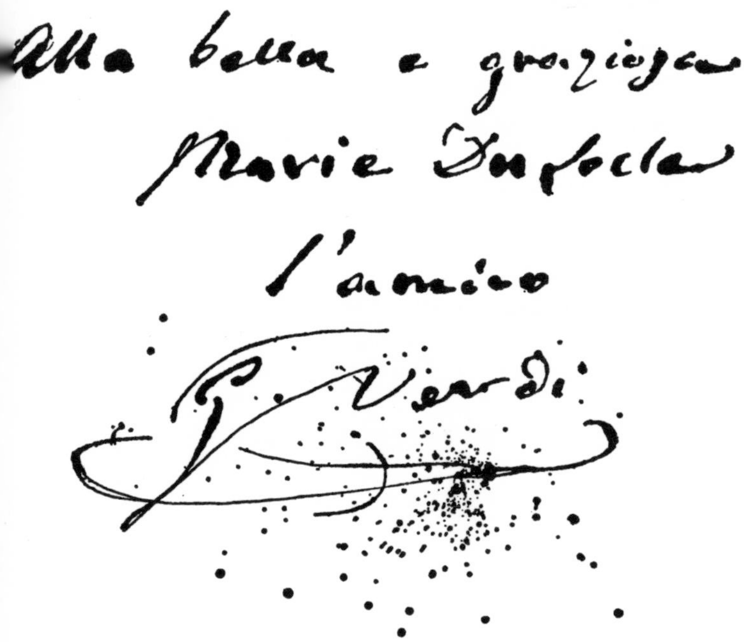

133

Speaking of Verdi, an art critic with a caustic wit once said: "Indecipherable music, tempered by illegible handwriting" (fig. 133).

The specimen shown here, complete with ink-blots, certainly does not suggest that his musical writing could have been entirely limpid! But how can a pen resist the impulsive passions of the man holding it? Just like his music, these thick letters, charged with all the driving emotions which Verdi put into musical form in his compositions, are an unbridled expression of his rich nature.

On some of the strokes in this specimen, the pen was almost pushed through the paper. The short shafts, the heavy, low punctuation, various heavy downstrokes and curves do not testify to great refinement of sentiment or marked spiritual qualities in their author. He is a man of passion, a man of action, a realist who immediately gets to the facts, with a sincerity and a generosity which can sometimes be quite brutal.

However, this hand is neither hard nor angular. The profile of a generous heart can be readily discerned under the outer layer of temperament—a heart which showed its feelings not only in Verdi's music, but also in his ardent patriotism.

Note particularly the series of curves, hooks and brackets which make up the flourish around Verdi's signature; this is his way of asserting himself in his own eyes, and also of protecting himself from the outer tumult. He did not like noise, and abhorred the publicity which surrounded his talent; he intended to triumph through his own merits alone.

134

Nobel

Nobel

This sample contains only five words, including two for the signature—which is not much to go on when analyzing a character. Yet the robust simplicity of the hand fully conveys the whole of his strong and winning personality (fig. 134).

This clear, smooth, full hand—rounded, but not soft, firm but not heavy—embodies an inquisitive mind, a man of positive accomplishments, and a balance of the finest human qualities.

The slope of the words follows the natural inclination of the hand, and reflects thought processes which move resolutely, but calmly, ahead.

In both loops and downstrokes—note particularly the three *y*'s—Nobel's positive willpower expresses itself strongly, yet without violence. Affirmation passes smoothly and confidently to the stage of practical achievement.

These five words contain no sign of selfishness, yet they are solidly rooted in the real world. Nobel's salient feature was his generosity, in his hard work as a scientist and inventor, in the zeal with which he made explosives available to man, and also—mingled with a tinge of remorse, perhaps—in the gift of his vast fortune to those same men to whom he had given a terrible instrument of destruction. This generosity stands out clearly from the handwriting in this specimen.

135

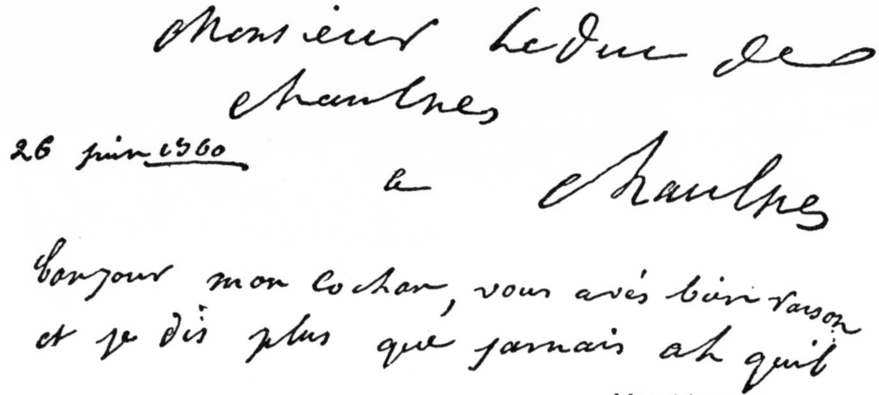
Monsieur le Duc de Chaulnes
26 juin 1760 a Chaulnes
Bonjour mon cochon, vous avés bien raison et je dis plus que jamais ah quil

Madame de Pompadour

Marchioness of Pompadour

In this letter, the favorite of Louis XV reveals the dominant features of her personality, from the very first stroke. Her sloping, semi-angular hand, lively but uneven, is evidence of the passion with which she set about satisfying her desires. The sharp barbed hooks and the lassoo-shaped final letters fittingly convey her overwhelming selfishness and her boundless ambitions.

In her quest for royal favor, Pompadour relied heavily on her wit, her quick and lively repartee and a positively cheeky candor.

This handwriting, with its alternating angles and rounded shapes, is curiously lacking in grace. Our beautiful schemer's idea of flirtatiousness had more provocation than coaxing in it; rather than feminity, she used an aggressive impatience in order to get her way.

Though lacking in gentleness, this hand is nonetheless not without sensitivity. This particular brand of sensitivity, however, is superficial, in that it is directed more towards the beautiful than the good, and the excessive selfishness and ambition of Pompadour could statisfy it only by draining funds from the State coffers, in order to indulge her taste for luxury.

Madame de Pompadour's handwriting suggests a personality somewhat different from that commonly attributed to her in history books; it does not indicate cunning, deviousness or low intrigue as dominant traits of her character.Rather, her strength lay in the passion and the logic with which she used her natural gifts and her charms to advance her cause; moreover, she skilfully drew on the weaknesses of others, in order to win or keep their favour.

Credits: Atlas, 16; Chabaud/Fotogram, 5, 7, 35; Chapuis/Atlas, 8; De Latour, 25; Fotogram, 83; Giraudon, 3, 51, 53, 69, 70; Phelps/Rapho, 12; Roger-Viollet, 11, 15, 19, 20a, 20b, 20c, 21a, 21b, 30, 32, 79, 80, 89, 99, 103, 104, 105, 106, 107, 108, 109, 111a, 111b, 113, 114a, 114b, 117b, 118; Scala, 52.